Life with the
QUEEN

BRIAN HOEY

SUTTON PUBLISHING

First published in 2006 by

Sutton Publishing Limited • Phoenix Mill

Thrupp • Stroud • Gloucestershire • GL5 2BU

British Library Cataloguing in Publication Data

A catalogue record for this book is available from the British Library.

ISBN 07509-4352-1

Title–page photograph: The Queen on a visit to Canada, April 2005. *(Fiona Hanson/PA/EMPICS)*

Typeset in 9.5/15.5 pt Eurostile.

Typesetting and origination by

Sutton Publishing Limited.

Printed and bound in England by

J.H. Haynes & Co. Ltd, Sparkford.

Contents

For my wife
Diana
in our golden wedding year

Acknowledgements

I am indebted to many people for their help in writing this book. Some asked not to be named for reasons of the confidentiality clauses in their terms of employment, others who spoke to me or helped me in their official capacity, include, in no particular order: Sir Robin Janvrin, Lt Col Sir Malcolm Ross, Vice-Admiral Tom Blackburn, Andrew Farquharson, Sir Hugh Roberts, David Rankin-Hunt, Sir Michael Oswald, Lady Angela Oswald, Penny Russell-Smith, Ailsa Anderson, David Pogson, Emma Copper, Pamela Clark and Lt Col Robert Cartwright, all of whom are present or past members of the Royal Household. Lord (David) Owen, Lord Carrington, the late Lord Callaghan, President George Bush Snr, President Gerald Ford, Dr Henry Kissinger and the former Prime Minister of Singapore, Mr Lee Kwan Yew, either answered my questions or allowed me to quote from their published writings, while Janice Robertson and June Spurgeon made valuable contributions to the manuscript. At Sutton Publishing, Jeremy Yates-Round, Jaqueline Mitchell, Alison Miles and Jane Entrican have been patient and encouraging for the past year, as have the photographers who provided the images and who are acknowledged elsewhere. Finally, my agent Ali Gunn at Curtis Brown is a non-stop bundle of energy who has worked tirelessly on my behalf. My thanks to them all. As usual, all opinions, unless quoted, are mine and mine alone.

The Queen admiring corgis outside the Alberta Legislature in Canada. (Paul Chiasson/Canada Press/EMPICS)

The Woman who is *The Queen*

Elizabeth II is the most famous woman in the world and yet arguably its most private. Her public image is recognised in every country on earth, but very few people know the person behind the regal smile, the courtly wave. We have all seen her in a variety of guises: dressed up in her formal robes at the State Opening of Parliament, the only time, apart from her Coronation, when she wears a crown; until 1986 in the scarlet uniform of the Brigade of Guards taking the salute at the Trooping the Colour Parade. Since that year, she has appeared in ordinary day clothes, as she no longer rides side-saddle to the parade at the head of her troops. We have watched her in the colourful cloak and bonnet of the Order of the Garter as she processes to St George's Chapel each June for the annual service of the Order, and some of us have been fortunate enough to see her at closer quarters in her own home when she acts as hostess to several thousand guests during one of the summer Garden Parties. Each image is different and each of us has a view about this woman who has been the Queen since 1952.

Those meeting her in person for the first time are surprised at how tiny she is. Seeing her on television, she appears to be of average height and weight; in person she is petite. While in repose she looks quite stern, when she smiles her face lights up, but she also gives the impression that she is rather shy. In fact, this is not so. She is supremely self-confident with not an ounce of doubt in her make-up. Her apparent shyness comes from the fact that she does not mind silences. If she has nothing to say she will remain mute. It can be off-putting to some people but it doesn't bother her in the slightest. She knows that wherever she goes she is the event, so even though she has the ability to put people at their ease, which she invariably does at the small luncheon parties she gives once a month at Buckingham Palace, she does not feel that awkward gaps in conversation have to be filled at all costs.

The Queen hasn't always been like this. As a young woman she was rather reserved, mainly because her mother insisted on holding centre stage and did not appreciate competition – even from her own children. But in her years as Sovereign she has grown in confidence to the point where today she is fully aware of her importance, without being self-important, and that she need not be overawed by anyone, no matter how elevated they may be. If she ever has an attack of nervousness, she manages to conceal it brilliantly and even when she visits countries with temperatures in the nineties, no one has ever seen her perspire. Whatever her secret is, it works for her. The Queen has rigid emotional self-control, a characteristic she inherited from her grandfather, King George V.

She has a natural dignity and an innate graciousness, even if she does not possess the combination of star quality and common touch that was unique to her late mother.

One of her longest-serving courtiers told me the reason why she sometimes appears cold is that she has the very English reserve that borders on indifference, and to some outsiders this is seen as arrogance, a characteristic she certainly does not possess. She is neither class-conscious, nor racially prejudiced. She treats everyone the same, no matter where they come from or from what station in life. She is as likely to stop and chat with one of her stable lads as with the Archbishop of Canterbury – probably more likely as they would have more in common. She bestows her friendship cautiously, but once given it is there for life and she regards loyalty as by far the most important of personal qualities.

Elizabeth II has been on the throne for more than half a century and in that time she has been served by eleven prime ministers, one of whom, Harold Wilson, served two separate terms of office, another, Margaret Thatcher, was the first and, so far, the only woman to hold the position, while Tony Blair was not even born when she acceded to the throne in

King George VI and Queen Elizabeth with their two daughters, Princess Elizabeth and Princess Margaret, photographed at Buckingham Palace shortly after the Coronation service in Westminster Abbey on 12 May 1937. (PA/EMPICS)

1952. Her first prime minister, Winston Churchill, who adored her, had been born in the reign of her great-great-grandmother, Queen Victoria, fought in the Boer War and had taken part in the last mounted cavalry charge made by the British Army.

Popes have come and gone during her reign; American presidents have been elected and defeated, and she has seen countless other heads of state come to office and be deposed. She is without doubt the most experienced stateswoman in the world, whose store of knowledge is unrivalled. She became Head of the Commonwealth by acclamation, not by right simply because she was Queen, and every single member of that eclectic group admits that she is the cement that holds the organisation together. Elizabeth was not born to be Queen as her father, the then Duke of York, was the second son of King George V and happily believed that his elder brother,

David, would succeed to the throne, marry and provide the country with the necessary heir. It was not to be. As we now know, David did become King Edward VIII, but only for nine months before abdicating in 1936 in order to marry the woman he loved, the American divorcee, Wallis Simpson.

So, not only did the life of his younger brother Albert change dramatically overnight, but the future of Albert's elder daughter Elizabeth was mapped out for the rest of her life. Had Edward VIII remained King and produced an heir, Elizabeth would today be merely an elderly aunt known as the Duchess of Edinburgh (if her husband had been elevated to the dukedom) far removed from the throne, and her mother, who died in 2002, would have held the title Duchess of York, not Queen Elizabeth the Queen Mother.

Prince Charles and Prince William would have been some way down the line of succession and media interest in their affairs would have been minimal. Prince Charles's affair and subsequent marriage to Camilla Parker Bowles, later Duchess of Cornwall, would never have aroused the worldwide interest it generated – or caused the rift in public opinion it provoked. It would have been merely a footnote in Royal history and not provided the headlines it did. Princess Diana would not have become the most photographed woman in the world and Sarah Ferguson would certainly not be the present Duchess of York.

Elizabeth was just 10 years and 8 months old when she learned her father was now King George VI, Emperor (the last) of India, and recognised as King in the Dominions of Australia, New Zealand, Canada and South Africa as well as being titular Head of the Empire on which, Britons were proud to boast, the sun never set. But even though to the young Princess Elizabeth the events of that momentous day caused barely a ripple in her everyday life, she had long been aware of the invisible wall that divided Royalty from commoner. Her paternal grandfather, King George V, whom she adored, together with his consort, Queen Mary, had instilled in her from the earliest age a belief that she and her little sister, Princess Margaret Rose, were different from everyone else.

Queen Mary did not believe that royalty – particularly girls – needed educating in any subjects other than history, so they would know their family background, and geography, in order to be able to point out on an atlas the countries they reigned over. French was also a requirement as it was still at that time the language of the Court, so both Elizabeth and Margaret learned to speak it when they were young children – even if, in later life, their accents leaned more towards upper-class English than aristocratic French.

George V was said to be the least formally educated monarch of the twentieth century and like his second son and eventually his elder granddaughter was not expected to be Sovereign when he was born. A year younger than his brother, Prince Albert Victor, Duke of Clarence and Avondale, it was when Albert (known in the family as Eddie) died of pneumonia in 1892, that Prince George became heir to the throne. He also inherited his late brother's fiancée, Princess Victoria Mary (May) of Teck, who was to become his Queen.

A hereditary monarchy is truly one of the great lotteries in that no one knows if the jackpot winner will be a suitable candidate for the top job. Queen Victoria despaired of her son Bertie, the gambling and womanising Prince of Wales. Yet he became, as Edward VII, one of the most successful and popular monarchs of the last 200 years. Similarly, his son, George V, who received the Crown by default, and who, on his own admission, preferred the quiet and ordered life of a country squire to the burdens of being a constitutional monarch, emerged as a leader of his people who was revered and respected, by politicians, foreign Heads of State, the British aristocracy and particularly by the ordinary men and women of Great Britain. If the choice had been his, he would have remained a career officer in the Royal Navy and throughout his life his humour reflected the broad appeal of a sailor's sense of fun. But when he came to the throne, he managed to overcome his initial distrust of ceremonial life and even endowed the office of monarchy with an extra layer of dignity, combined with an intuitive instinct for the feelings of the less advantaged of his subjects. His reign of a quarter of a century saw massive changes in the social structure of the world and he became an inspired leader of his people during the First World War when he endured the horror of hundreds of thousands of men being killed on the battlefields of Flanders.

When he died in 1936 the nation and the empire mourned with genuine grief. But there was hope that the new King, Edward VIII, would bring prosperity and vitality to the country. Edward VIII had been a charismatic and ultra-popular Prince of Wales. Handsome, debonair and acclaimed as the most eligible bachelor in the world, he was seen by the populace as the brightest star in the Royal firmament – except by his mother, Queen Mary, and his immediate family and certain leading public figures, who realised that he had feet of clay.

Within months of his accession he had decided to relinquish his responsibilities and abandon the throne. The Abdication caused the biggest constitutional crisis the country and empire had ever known. There were such major divisions in Britain – between those who supported Edward and believed he should have been permitted to remain on the throne and still marry Wallis Simpson, and those who were adamant that the King must make a choice: duty or personal happiness – that the guards outside Buckingham Palace were issued with live ammunition on Abdication Day for the first and only time, just in case the crowds attempted to rush the Palace.

On the day that her father became King George VI, the 10-year-old Princess Elizabeth remained at the family home at 145 Piccadilly, where the Four Seasons Hotel now stands without even a plaque on the wall to commemorate the fact that it was once the site of The Queen's London home.

Three years after Princess Elizabeth became heir presumptive, the Second World War broke out. She was 13. By the time it ended in 1945 she was a 19-year-old subaltern in the ATS (women's Auxiliary Territorial Service), having learned how to drive and maintain motor vehicles, including 3-ton trucks. She claims she can still change a carburettor with her eyes closed. However, her father refused to allow her to live in the quarters allocated to her fellow officers in the Army, saying it would compromise her Royal status if she were seen to be sharing accommodation with women who were commoners. Instead she had to suffer the indignity of having to return every night to sleep in her own bed at Windsor Castle. One of the young women who served with the Princess at the time told me recently that they were under strict orders not to confuse friendliness with familiarity:

Most of us had been warned in advance that she was joining us and we were told in no uncertain terms that under no circumstances were we to try and get too close to her. Some days we spent hours under a lorry or with our heads buried inside an oily engine and we would emerge filthy dirty and covered in grease. So we would head straight for the showers – all except Princess Elizabeth. She never undressed in front of us – even for what we called an 'all-over wash'. Her batwoman was in constant attendance and I cannot recall the Princess ever looking as if she needed a bath. None of us ever saw her in her underwear so we didn't even get a glimpse of the Royal knickers. While the rest of us mucked in together, Princess Elizabeth was carefully segregated from us. I don't think it was her idea, she was always quite relaxed in our company, but our senior officers were never far away and they all 'walked on egg shells' when she was around. The one thing I can remember is that when we had a break for a cigarette, she always joined in. She enjoyed a smoke as much as any of us. The other thing is that her uniforms were better tailored than ours, and even her overalls were laundered and pressed every day.

The Princess's military service lasted only for a few weeks but at least it gave her a taste of what passes – in royalty's terms – for normal living and The Queen herself has said that the last time she felt 'one of the crowd' was on VE (Victory in Europe) night when she and Princess Margaret sneaked out of Buckingham Palace – with, it has to be admitted, a couple of equerries in tow – to mingle with the tens of thousands gathered outside the Palace gates shouting for the King and Queen to appear. His Majesty later said, when he was told of the episode, 'Poor darlings, they haven't had much fun.'

The year of 1947 was the next milestone in Elizabeth's life. The King had reluctantly given his consent for his beloved daughter to be married to Lieutenant Philip Mountbatten, a distant cousin; they could both trace direct lines back to Queen Victoria. Elizabeth was 21 years old, Philip five years older, handsome and distinguished-looking, who had served in the Royal Navy with distinction during the war. The King's reluctance to give his permission for them to marry had been for several reasons. Philip was not out of the top draw of European royalty, the Greek royal

Second Lieutenant HRH The Princess Elizabeth servicing an Austin 10 while serving with No. 1 MTTC at Camberley, Surrey in 1945 towards the end of the Second World War. The Queen says she could still change a carburettor if she had to. (PA/EMPICS)

family languishing somewhere near the bottom of the league table. Neither did he possess a great fortune or estates to bring into the family. There was also severe opposition from some of the King's most senior advisers who felt Philip was too rough and ready for the delicate protocol of life at Court. They were proved right as soon as Elizabeth became Queen, as Philip went through the Palace like a dose of salts sweeping away outmoded practices that had existed unchallenged for generations.

However, Elizabeth showed she too had steel in her spine and eventually the King gave way and she and Philip were married in Westminster Abbey on a cold, wet November day in 1947, the year that would see the coldest winter of the century. For the first five years of their marriage, the Royal couple lived an idyllic existence. Clarence House was their first proper home and when Philip, who had remained on active service with the Royal Navy, was posted to Malta, his wife went with him. Two children were born: Charles in 1948 followed by his sister Anne in 1950.

But it all came to an end in 1952. Elizabeth and Philip were in Kenya at the start of an official tour when they were told that King George VI had died at Sandringham. He was 56. So at the age of 25, Elizabeth Alexandra Mary, the first child of King George VI and his consort, Queen Elizabeth, became the forty-second Sovereign of England since William the Conqueror, yet only the sixth Queen Regnant.

She is now the longest-reigning British monarch since Queen Victoria, who was the last Queen Regnant, and who reigned for sixty-three years, while their joint ancestor, Elizabeth I, reigned for forty-four years. Elizabeth II is also the first female Sovereign to bear the family name of Windsor, which was adopted by her grandfather, King George V, in 1917 to avoid accusations during the First World War that the monarchy was German.

The Queen was crowned in Westminster Abbey on 2 June 1953 when her full titles were revealed as: Elizabeth the Second, by the Grace of God, of the United Kingdom of Great Britain and Northern Ireland and of her other Realms and Territories Queen, Head of the Commonwealth, Defender of the Faith. She was not, and never was to become, Empress, as India, from where the title was taken, had been granted independence in 1947, the year she was married.

In the fifty-odd years she has been on the throne, The Queen has never put a foot wrong in her public or private life. She is an affectionate wife,

Her Majesty The Queen with her seven maids of honour after the Coronation service on 2 June 1953. They are from left to right: Lady Moyra Hamilton; Lady Rosemary Spencer-Churchill; Lady Anne Coke; Lady Jane Heathcote-Drummond-Willoughby; Lady Jane Vane-Tempest-Stewart; Lady Mary Baillie-Hamilton and, standing next to The Queen, the Mistress of the Robes, the Dowager Duchess of Devonshire. (PA/EMPICS)

loving mother (with two more children, Andrew and Edward, being born while she was Queen) and devoted grandparent, characteristics that have never impinged on her devotion to duty. This is the quality she possesses above all others. In many ways she has sacrificed a normal family life to the demands of public office. Her closest friends say it was a tragedy that she and Philip could not have shared longer as a normal married couple instead of having to don the mantle of constitutional monarchy at such an early age, together with responsibilities that have taken precedence over all else. And never once has she shirked those duties, as irksome as many must be. She has served her country with dignity and devotion and has borne the marital problems of her late sister, and three of her children, with fortitude.

A very private woman by inclination, she has been forced to live most of her life in the full glare of public attention. It is not a position she has found to her liking, but one she has accepted with grace and dignity, or, as Prince Philip has said, 'It goes with the job.' Her Majesty's reign has been the most informal of Britain's 1,000-year monarchy and she has made herself more accessible than any of her distinguished predecessors through her television and radio broadcasts. It has taken her years to come to terms with the intrusive television cameras but her natural good nature and honest approach shine through on each occasion. The one time she does not emerge as someone speaking from the heart is when she reads The Queen's Speech from the House of Lords at the State Opening of Parliament. The reason is that every word is written for her by the prime minister of the day, and she is required to read it word for word with no changes.

As a constitutional monarch the powers of The Queen are, in theory, awesome. All wars are declared in her name, as are negotiations for peace. She is Commander-in-Chief of all the British Armed Forces: Army, Navy and Royal Air Force, and could, again in theory, disband the forces and sell all the military equipment: ships, aircraft and tanks, if she so wished. When it was decided to downgrade the rank of the officer who commanded the former Royal Yacht, *Britannia*, from an admiral – as it had always been – to a mere commodore, a member of Her Majesty's family mischievously suggested that she should promote him to admiral, which, as Commander-in-Chief, she was perfectly entitled to do. The Queen replied wistfully: 'Oh. If only I dared.' Of course, as Britain is a democracy with an elected government none of these things could take place in practice. But The Queen remains the Fount of Honour, conferring knighthoods and peerages, again usually on the 'advice' of her prime minister, and all foreign emissaries are accredited to her Court of St James's. So while her direct political powers are strictly limited, her influence in political matters is immense.

In 1991, President Ronald Reagan succinctly summed up the attitude and feelings of many people when he said, 'Throughout the world, with all due respect to every other female monarch, whenever we speak about "The Queen" we all know which one we are referring to.' He was right. Elizabeth II is unique; the acceptable face of what to some is an outmoded institution, and even those who disagree with everything she stands for admit, perhaps grudgingly, that she has earned widespread respect and admiration as one of the most remarkable individuals in the world.

Invitation to *the Palace*

The Queen and Prince Philip are 'working the room' at Buckingham Palace. All is going according to plan, as it invariably does at Royal functions. Her Majesty and Prince Philip are greeting their guests with smiles and words of welcome in the genteel manner expected of Royalty when Prince Andrew, Duke of York, who is supporting his parents this evening, sees a familiar face across the room. All protocol is forgotten as he runs to meet the woman he has recognised. Throwing both arms around her, he lifts her in the air and gives her a kiss on both cheeks, before turning to acknowledge her husband standing quietly at her side. The lady is Cherie Blair, the self-styled 'First Lady' of Downing Street; her husband is, of course, the Prime Minister, resplendent in white tie and tails. The guests standing either side of them look on with great amusement – and a little envy – at the obvious familiarity between The Queen's second son and the wife of the nation's most important man. Mrs Blair blushes but does not curtsy – neither does she when she is presented to Her Majesty.

For most of the people present this is the occasion of a lifetime, when they get to meet and talk to The Queen and Prince Philip on a personal basis. For Her Majesty, it is just another evening when she opens her doors to several hundred men and women. On this occasion, they are the great and good from all over the world, diplomats who are based in

London, and the reception is The Queen's way of showing her appreciation of their presence in Britain.

It's not easy being the nation's hostess; having to offer hospitality to thousands of men and women every year, the majority of whom you never meet or with whom you cannot possibly have anything in common. But The Queen has enjoyed – if that's the right word – this dubious privilege ever since she came to the throne in 1952, and never once has she shirked the responsibility even when she has felt like doing so, shaking hands with up to 500 people at a time and standing – she never sits at a Palace function unless it is a sit-down dinner – for hours on end, when all she probably wants is to kick off her shoes and put her feet up, and perhaps watch one of her favourite programmes on television. It is an integral part of being a constitutional monarch; throwing open your doors to those the government of the day has decided should be invited to the Palace, and also welcoming smaller, more intimate groups the Household feels it would be beneficial for the Sovereign to meet. For The Queen it's all in a day's work.

At least two State Banquets are held at Buckingham Palace each year to mark visits by foreign Heads of State. In 2004 there were three: Poland, France and Korea; in 2005, just two: Norway and China. The visits all last the same amount of time: four days, regardless of the size and importance of the country. At Buckingham Palace all Heads of State are accommodated in the three-roomed Belgian Suite on the ground floor, with French windows opening onto the terrace leading across to the garden. Named after King Leopold I of the Belgians – an uncle and great favourite of Queen Victoria – it is where both of The Queen's youngest children, Andrew and Edward, were born.

The largest of the three rooms is the Eighteenth-century Room hung with magnificent paintings by Gainsborough, Canaletto and Zuccarelli. Next door is the Orleans Room, the main bedroom, where the colour scheme is entirely blue and where three portraits of Queen Victoria occupy places of honour. The third and smallest of the rooms in the Belgian Suite is the Spanish Room, which can be used as a bedroom if required but is more often used as a dressing room. If the visiting Head of State requires a private dining room, he or she is offered the Carnarvon Room, which, though not strictly a part of the Belgian Suite, is close by.

The Master of the Household told me that The Queen takes a personal interest in the welfare and comfort of her guests and always visits the suite before a Head of State arrives to make sure everything is in order. She chooses the flowers to decorate the rooms and makes suggestions about little things like the books that should be placed alongside the beds.

The State Banquet takes place on the first evening when the Duke of Edinburgh collects the Head of State from the Belgian Suite and conducts him or her to the Royal Closet, a small drawing room on the first floor, hidden behind the White Drawing Room, where The Queen is waiting and where the Royal Family and their house guests enjoy a private pre-dinner drink.

If the State Visit is being held at Windsor Castle, as was the case when Nelson Mandela, Ronald Reagan and President Chirac were Her Majesty's guests, they will stay in the principal guest apartment, number 240, overlooking the Long Walk towards Ascot Racecourse. This apartment has a bedroom, two bathrooms (one each for the principal guest and his or her spouse) and a sitting room. A footman and maid are attached to the visiting suite and a plentiful supply of whisky, brandy and gin is laid on, with the Yeoman of the Royal Cellars being informed in advance about the guests' favourite brands.

To each of the State Banquets some 170 guests are invited (136 at Windsor because St George's Hall is smaller than the State Ballroom at Buckingham Palace) and the form never changes: the Foreign Office makes the formal arrangements about who is to be asked and, in conjunction with the Master of the Household, also arranges the seating plan for the evening. This has to be carried out in accordance with strict order of precedence and Royal protocol. The final word always rests with Her Majesty and this is by no means simply a matter of her rubber-stamping everything that is placed in front of her. She will ask searching questions about the proposed guest list, particularly if she does not know why such and such a person has been included or where they are located.

The Master has a large table plan in his office and he and his staff juggle with the proposed guest list until they get it right. They use colour-coded cards, with red being reserved for the Royal Family (except for The Queen who does not have a place card) and blue for the visiting entourage. In this way they are able to arrange the seating accordingly. Once the table plan has been finalised it is printed in a small booklet containing the name of every guest and inside the back cover is a diagram of the table showing where everyone is seated.

The difficulty for The Queen is that even if she wanted to, she cannot invite anyone she likes. There are matters of protocol to be observed and while she rarely tries to countermand the 'advice' offered to her by Downing Street and the Foreign Office, she does have a way of showing her disapproval when guests are invited whom she actively dislikes. She still allows them to be presented, but they do not get more than a couple of seconds in the Royal presence, without a word being exchanged, and she quickly moves on to the next person in the line-up.

Of the 170 or so guests at any of the official State Banquets, the majority are there because of their rank or position. The Prime Minister and their spouse are invited on every occasion. So too is the Leader of the Opposition and the leaders of other major political parties. The Foreign Secretary and ministers of state are included and the Archbishop of Canterbury and his wife are also on every guest list. Then there is the ambassador or High Commissioner who represents the country being honoured with the banquet and several members of his entourage. If it is a Commonwealth country, the Secretary-General, who is based at nearby Marlborough House, is another 'must have' on the list.

Private invitations usually are extended to people who have a particular connection with the visiting Head of State or their country. They may be businessmen with commercial interests or people who have performed a service, especially if it is in a developing country. Members of The Queen's Household make up the remainder of the table plan, interspersed with the official guests at intervals so they can help the evening go with a swing and perhaps converse about the Palace and its history to those who are visiting for the first and possibly only time in their lives.

The menus are planned months in advance in conjunction with the embassy or High Commission. Any particular dietary requirements are

Opposite: A State Banquet, either at Buckingham Palace or Windsor Castle – where this one was held in honour of France's President Chirac – is a glittering occasion, with the Royal Family and their guests wearing 'every rock in the book'. The Queen always sits at the centre of the table and no one has to ask for the salt and pepper to be passed – there's a set of condiments beside every place-setting. (John Stillwell/PA/EMPICS)

catered for, with special care taken if the guest of honour comes from a country where alcohol is banned and where certain meats are not eaten. The Royal chef knows from long experience that Her Majesty likes her meat to be extra well done so he places a sprig of parsley on her plate to distinguish it from all the others. Guests have been known to hide a pat of butter as a souvenir of the banquet as they are all stamped with a tiny crown. This is not wise as when they are placed in pockets or handbags the butter will have melted by the time the guests reach home.

The Queen, as hostess, has the final word on every aspect of the function, from the details of which of her many priceless dinner services and gold cutlery – and it is solid gold (she once famously remarked, 'People don't come here because of the food; they come to eat off gold plates') – will be used, down to the flower arrangements and the music to be played during the evening by the band of the Household Brigade who will be on duty in the gallery above the ballroom.

Nothing is left to chance and when the tables are being laid, the Palace Steward, the senior of Her Majesty's domestic servants, measures each place setting and the distance between each one with a ruler. There's a very practical reason for what seems at first glance to be a rather fussy practice; if he didn't measure the distances accurately, he might get to the end of the table and find they were a couple of places short. Even though he has carried out this procedure scores of times, the Palace Steward still goes through the same routine before every banquet. That is why Royal functions are organised to operate like clockwork. Nothing is taken for granted; everything is checked and checked again and again. Each chair is placed precisely 27 inches from the table, which is 160 feet (48 metres) long in a horseshoe shape that takes six men 3 hours to assemble. They use 1,350 knives, forks and spoons with 850 pure crystal glasses (five for each place setting: sherry, white wine, red wine, champagne and water, another for port is added towards the end of the meal).

The banquets always start at 8.30 p.m. with guests beginning to arrive for drinks at 7 p.m. They always finish by midnight and guests who might try to overstay their welcome by hanging around hoping for another drink, suddenly find the footmen have disappeared and so have the drinks. Guests at State Banquets sometimes marvel at the sheer theatricality of this Royal event, but the fact that the Palace Steward and his team have performed this countless

Work begins at 6 a.m. when staff are preparing for a reception or State Banquet and even though they have all done it many times before nothing is left to chance because there is only one standard of Royal hospitality – perfection. (By permission of Buckingham Palace)

times before is the reason why it all appears so effortless. They believe in the old boxing adage 'Train hard and fight easy.' The Queen has provided the venue and acted as a gracious hostess while the Foreign Office has picked up the bill, which for each State Banquet is around £12,000.

By far the most glittering occasion in the Royal calendar is the Diplomatic Reception given by Her Majesty every November at Buckingham Palace. It always takes place on a Wednesday evening and it is strictly white tie, decorations and tails, or, as one of the Royal Household puts it, 'They wear every rock in the book.' Moss Bros., the specialists in hiring out full-dress evening wear, starts taking orders months before the big event and the idea of any guest being seen in anything as mundane as a mere dinner jacket and black tie is unthinkable. For the ladies, it is full-length ball gowns, with colourful national dress often worn by guests of both sexes.

The Diplomatic Reception is easily the largest and most important social gathering of the season with a total of 1,298 guests representing the

160 foreign missions based in London. It is physically impossible to invite every member of every mission, so the invitations are sent out on a sliding scale with the biggest mission, that of the United States, receiving the lion's share, while some of the smaller missions, such as Fiji, getting only a handful.

The reception is organised by the Master of the Household and his team who start their preparations a month before the event. The first thing they do is plan the menu, cost it so that it fits the budget they have been allocated and then send the menu upstairs to The Queen for her approval. Once she has done this – and she does sometimes make suggestions of her own – it then goes to the purchasing department in the Master's office. They enter it into the computer system that governs almost every aspect of Palace life these days, which then produces a shopping list of what they need to buy to achieve the required result.

The food is superb but fairly simple, consisting of two main courses, chicken and vegetarian, so it is very rare for a guest to find he or she

EIIR

The Lord Chamberlain
is commanded by Her Majesty to invite

....

....

to an Evening Reception at Buckingham Palace
on Wednesday, 10th November 2004
at 8.30 p.m.

National Dress or Evening Dress, Decorations
Uniform for Service Attachés

The most sought-after and prized invitation of the year, to the annual Diplomatic Reception, when representatives of every foreign embassy or High Commission in London are asked to meet The Queen and full evening dress or national costume is required. (Author's Collection)

cannot eat what's on offer. Experience has shown this method seems to work quite well.

As the reception is on a Wednesday, the purchasing orders for food are placed so that delivery can take place on the previous Friday, in order that the kitchen can start preparing on the following Monday with a view to having it all ready by the Wednesday afternoon. It is arranged with military-like precision so that on the day itself, the food is ready at 6.20 p.m., loaded into hot cupboards by 6.45, moved up to the ballroom, where the buffet is laid out, by 7 p.m., which means that all is ready by 7.05 when the guests start arriving.

The Household find it would be too difficult to feed all the guests at the same time so the invitations give two different times for the recipients to arrive at the Palace. The first group come in at 7 p.m. and the second at 8. Neither group realises that they have been asked to arrive at a time different from the other. Another reason for the splitting up of the 1,298 guests is that when The Queen joins the party, she meets the second group first – while the first are eating – and when they take their turn to eat she then meets the people who arrived at 7. It sounds complicated but so far experience has shown that this is the only way to fit everybody in – and it does work.

The catering operation involves meals for not only the guests but also for the staff. Andrew Farquharson, who is assistant to the Master of the Household 'F' Branch which handles, as its initial implies, all the Palace food requirements, explains how on the day of the reception everybody is fed. 'We start in the kitchens at 6.30 in the morning, cooking breakfast for the staff who are on duty at 7 a.m. Then we provide lunch for about 400 before starting on the preparations for the evening. We actually produce about 3,000 portions because as it's a buffet you never really know what everyone is going to have so you cook more of everything – and quite often people decide to have a bit of everything and so far we have never run out of food. We'll also be cooking staff suppers for around 200/250, so all in all by the time the day is over we will have produced something in the region of 3,700 meals.'

For a State Banquet, extra footmen are hired for the evening, but for the Diplomatic Reception, which has ten times the number of guests, only four catering students are brought in, usually a fortnight before, in order to give them a little work experience and to use the extra pairs of hands for the

The kitchens at Buckingham Palace are run with military-like precision, with up to 600 meals a day being prepared when a major function is planned. The Queen likes to claim that much of the food eaten in the Palace has been grown or reared on the Royal estates. (By permission of Buckingham Palace)

more basic tasks. A stint in the Buckingham Palace kitchens also does them no harm when it appears on their CVs.

The kitchens at Buckingham Palace are on the lower ground floor and are the domain of the Royal Chef, Mark Flemington, who oversees the nineteen chefs in the main kitchen. As zero hour approaches there is a tremendous flurry of activity, but while it is certainly frenetic, there is no panic. Mark Flemington knows exactly what he is doing and every member of each brigade (that's the name they give the cooking teams) is equally efficient. Robert, the pastry chef, has a reputation for being something of an ultra perfectionist, but apparently that's the norm for pastry chefs, four of whom are preparing dessert next door to the main kitchen.

The atmosphere below stairs is quite amazing. It's like a scene from 100–150 years ago with various people in different states of Court dress hanging around waiting for the big event to start. There are footmen in their scarlet tunics, complete with any decorations they are entitled to wear; butlers in white tie and tails with miniature medals; junior footmen in knee breeches, and just outside in the inner courtyard a couple of dismounted troopers of the Household Cavalry in thigh boots and spurs, having a quiet puff on their cigarettes before they go inside just before The Queen makes an appearance, ready to stand guard for 3 hours. There is also a queue at the lavatories just before the main event.

Because the reception provides only a buffet-style meal, several members of the Royal Household, who live nearby in grace and favour apartments, host small dinner parties of their own before the main event. The most prestigious is that of the Lord Chamberlain, who occupies an elegant apartment in St James's Palace. He asks around twenty or so guests, including the Prime Minister, the Archbishop of Canterbury and their wives to join him and then – on fine evenings – they walk the short distance through Stable Yard, using the private Milkmaids Passage into Green Park to arrive at Buckingham Palace in plenty of time for the reception.

There are nineteen State Apartments at Buckingham Palace and all are brought into use for the Diplomatic Reception. When the first guests arrive they are gently guided towards the State Ballroom where the food has been laid out on tables arranged along the length of the room. They then move with their plates into two of the other State Apartments – the Blue and White Drawing Rooms – where they eat standing up as most of the

furniture has been removed to make room for them all. Once all the guests are safely inside the drawing rooms, the doors from the East Gallery are closed, enabling the tables to be cleared and reset ready for the next group. As soon as they move into the State Ballroom the ladies and

During the afternoon prior to the Diplomatic Reception held every November, the Royal florists, assisted by footmen, prepare hundreds of flower arrangements before they are transferred to decorate the State Apartments.
(By permission of Buckingham Palace)

gentlemen who have already eaten move towards the Picture Gallery, Throne Room and Green Drawing Room, where they will wait until The Queen and the rest of the Royal party arrive.

It is a magical sight. A cross between something from *The Arabian Nights* and the Ascot scene in *My Fair Lady*. Every national dress imaginable, every colour, race and creed, together with The Queen's extra equerries – all of whom appear to be over 6 feet tall and immaculate in full evening dress – brought in to ease the path of those guests who might feel slightly intimidated at their first meeting with the Sovereign or their first sight of Buckingham Palace.

Then the big moment arrives. A door opens and the figure of The Queen appears. She is wearing a shimmering, lavender, beaded full-length evening gown, topped with a glittering tiara. She looks magnificent.

The Duke of Edinburgh, still sprightly at 80-plus, if now a little stooped, and the Prince of Wales and the Duke of York accompany her. All three are wearing formal Court dress with silk stockings and decorations. The Master of the Diplomatic Corps, who is responsible for all matters of protocol among the diplomatic community, is on hand to present the various representatives to Her Majesty. The Head of the Royal Household, the Lord Chamberlain, and his Comptroller are also in evidence to help identify those guests who are being presented. They move among the crowd slightly ahead of the Royal party and ask if a particular person has met either The Queen or Prince Philip before. If they have, when their turn comes, they are introduced to Her Majesty with the words, 'This is . . . whom of course you already know.' The Queen then shakes hands and says how nice it is to see them again. In all probability she won't remember them; it is highly unlikely with the thousands of people she meets every year, but it is very flattering to the guest and makes them feel rather special – which is the whole idea.

It all looks fairly informal and spontaneous but, in fact, every move has been planned. There is even a map of the route the Royal party will take and the time The Queen and Prince Philip will spend in each room. This is circulated to everyone involved in the event but no one actually keeps it in their hands. It is surreptitiously tucked away in coat pockets and glanced at carefully when no one else is looking.

The Queen never hurries, spending just about the same amount of time with each person she meets; yet she arrives at the right spot at precisely the correct time in the evening. She does not go into the ballroom for any food; neither does she drink anything during the evening, though in all probability she will have had a gin and tonic before beginning her marathon evening. Prince Philip sticks to whisky.

As the Royal party moves from room to room, those who have been presented go to collect their food; it's a bit of a merry-go-round, but a highly civilised one. In the Ball Supper Room, which is not used for supper this evening, an orchestra has been set up and music for dancing begins. It's all middle-of-the-road: foxtrots and waltzes, with the occasional rumba, but none of the more modern dances where partners don't even touch each other, not even the twist. Again, something of a throwback to pre-war days. The footmen carry trays laden with champagne, whisky and gin, but if a guest asks for something a little more exotic, they will usually find it.

If there is one word to sum up the atmosphere of the Diplomatic Reception it is excitement. Everyone, the staff, Household and guests, is imbued with a special excitement that the evening generates. As Andrew Farquharson remarks, 'It is the most glamorous event of the year and I think if we and the team are excited by it then the guests pick up the vibes. If we went around looking as miserable as sin, they would soon pick that up as well, so if we're smiling, everybody smiles. All we want them to do is have a good time.'

By midnight everyone has gone and the job of clearing up begins. They never leave it until the next morning as there may well be another event planned. The ballroom is used for twenty-two Investitures every year and members of the Royal Family hold private lunches and dinners almost weekly, so the footmen and cleaners work for a couple of hours and everything is back to normal by 2 a.m. It's been a long day; starting at 6.30 for some of them and tomorrow they will have to be on duty again at 7 a.m. But the Master of the Household can look back on a job well done and his team know they are appreciated – by him and, more importantly, by The Queen.

An infinitely smaller and even more exclusive function is held at Windsor Castle every June to celebrate the Duke of Wellington's victory over Napoleon in 1815. Known as the Waterloo Banquet, the guest of honour is the present Duke of Wellington, who presents to Her Majesty a small silk tricolour flag, the annual rent for Stratfield Saye, his estate in Hampshire, which was given to the original Duke by a grateful nation. Only fifty-two guests sit down to the banquet and The Queen knows every one personally.

A few days earlier she has hosted another meal, this time a luncheon (The Queen never uses the diminutive 'lunch', thinking it vulgar) for the Knights of the Garter and their spouses. It precedes the annual Garter Service at which new knights are installed and the guest list includes those members of the Royal Family who are Knights or Ladies of the Garter and also foreign royalty who have been installed as Extra Knights. In spite of the impressive array of royalty and aristocracy, those who attend say it is so enjoyable because of the informality.

Once a month The Queen holds a luncheon party at Buckingham Palace for about a dozen guests, but this is usually a semi-business event as those invited are there because they may be able to contribute something towards The Queen's vast store of knowledge. It is an eclectic guest list with, perhaps, the head of the prison service, a pop singer, an eminent scientist, an actor and an author being included. But no politicians. The list has been drawn up by the Private Secretary in consultation with other members of the Household and submitted to Her Majesty for her approval.

The first the guests know that The Queen is approaching is when several of her corgis run into the room. One or two guests, thinking they will find favour with their hostess, bend down to fondle the dogs, only to be told sharply 'Don't do that please. They only respond to me.' She is right. The corgis only obey their Royal mistress and they have been known to nip at strange ankles during a visit. This luncheon is a short affair lasting just an hour and a half and The Queen brings it to a halt as soon as the time is up. For her it is purely a duty function, not one to be enjoyed at leisure.

Forty thousand men and women are invited to join Her Majesty every summer at one of her Garden Parties. There are three held in the grounds of Buckingham Palace in July, with another at the Palace of Holyroodhouse in Edinburgh when The Queen is in residence in the Scottish capital. In 2005, the Scottish Garden Party was moved back to the end of July in order not to clash with the demonstrators gathering in Edinburgh prior to the G8 Heads of Government meeting.

The Scottish Garden Party is a great favourite with Her Majesty who loves the skirl of the pipe bands that play during the afternoon, and she is attended by her Household in Scotland, headed by the Duke of Argyll, whose family has traditionally held the post for generations. The Duke of Hamilton and Brandon is Hereditary Keeper of the Palace of Holyroodhouse and the most colourful of her bodyguards, the Royal Company of Archers, clad in Sherwood green with feathered bonnets and clutching long bows (which they have paid for themselves) led by their Captain General, and the High Constables of Holyroodhouse, wearing distinctive blue uniforms and cockaded silk bonnets approved by The Queen's grandfather, King George V, in 1914, are always on duty at the Garden Party. It is the highlight of the Scottish season, with the 'great and the good' prominent among the guests, but invitations are also extended to many other 'ordinary' people who may have performed a service, either to the Sovereign or to the community.

The setting for the Garden Party is far more romantic than in London, with the ruins of the Abbey overlooked by Arthur's Seat all adding to the atmosphere. The kilts and tartans on show are also much more colourful than the formal morning dress seen at the Buckingham Palace event, so it seems to be a more relaxed affair altogether. And The Queen and the Duke of Edinburgh are able to meet more of their guests, so they appear more at ease.

In London, so many people accept their invitations that they have three separate entrances to the Garden Party: two directly into the 45-acre garden and one through the main entrance of the Palace, which most people use as it may be the only opportunity they get of seeing part of the inside.

At 4 p.m. precisely the doors to the terrace are locked as The Queen and Prince Philip move through the Bow Room and wait at the top of the steps while the national anthem is played. Any guest arriving late who has not managed to get into the garden by this time has to remain inside the Palace until the anthem has ended. The Queen and other members of the Royal Family who are on duty divide up and each one takes a separate line that has been formed by the crowds. It is easy to see which line The Queen is taking, as this is the only one protected by members of the Yeomen of the Guard.

As Her Majesty progresses towards her destination, which is the Royal Tea Marquee, her aides have preceded her and selected those men and women who are to be presented. They are brought out of the crowd, having told the courtier who they are and why they were invited, so when The Queen arrives the member of the Household presents them by name and occupation. The Queen spends a few minutes chatting and then moves on. No one gets more than the allotted time and even though The Queen never hurries she invariably arrives at the Tea Marquee at exactly the same moment as the other members of her family.

Inside the marquee, which is reserved for VIP guests, The Queen is handed a cup of tea but nothing to eat. She has never been seen to eat anything at any of these affairs and she only accepts the tea to put her guests at ease. A semicircle of 'ordinary' guests watch from a distance as the Royals take their tea. They cannot approach too near as a detachment of the Yeomen of the Guard is on duty to prevent anyone without the right ticket from entering the marquee.

Finally, The Queen and the other Royals disappear and the event is over. Some guests hover expectantly hoping to see her once more but they are disappointed and the staff quickly start to remove the plates, cups and saucers ready for a repeat of the exercise a few days later. In a little over 2 hours the guests have each consumed up to fourteen cakes, sandwiches

and ice creams and drunk four cups of tea or iced coffee. The annual bill for the Garden Parties is approximately £500,000.

A much more sought-after and more intimate invitation is to 'Dine and Sleep' at Windsor Castle – never at Buckingham Palace. These take place around four times a year when The Queen is in residence at Windsor and they date back to the reign of Queen Victoria. The idea is for The Queen to meet a few people in an informal setting, though the invitations indicate that 'black ties' will be worn.

The Master of the Household, after discussions with The Queen, sends out the invitations some four weeks before the event in question. Usually, six married couples and four single men and women are asked to arrive on a Friday evening between 6.30 and 7 p.m. They are met by a senior member of the Royal Household who conducts them to their rooms in the private wing of the Castle where a footman/valet and housemaid are waiting to unpack their suitcases. Baths are run for them during which any pressing of clothes that may be needed is done.

When they are dressed the guests are shown into the Green Drawing Room for drinks with their hostess and her husband. They can have anything they want; to date the Yeoman of the Royal Cellars has yet to be asked for something he cannot provide. This is the first time the guests meet each other and also The Queen and the Duke of Edinburgh. Dinner is served at 8.30 and

Royal Garden Parties are held three times a year at Buckingham Palace with a further one at the Palace of Holyroodhouse in Edinburgh. Guests who are to be presented to The Queen are singled out by a member of the Royal Household and asked to stand a little way in front of the main body.
(Fiona Hanson/PA/EMPICS)

the only formality is that the principal male guest always escorts The Queen with the Duke taking the arm of the guest's wife – if he is married. As with every Royal meal, a seating plan has been arranged previously with The Queen's approval so that all the guests are within talking range of a member of the Royal Family or Household, and no one has to wait to be spoken to, as they would have done in previous reigns.

When Neil (now Lord) Kinnock, the former Leader of the Labour Party and subsequently European Commissioner, and his wife Glenys, a Member of the European Parliament, were guests, they found the occasion highly entertaining and not in the least intimidating. 'Prince Philip broke the ice straight away and we had a good old argument about rugby. It seemed to me that the more I disagreed with him, the better we got on.'

Once the meal is finished, The Queen takes her guests on a personally conducted tour of those parts of the Castle not normally open to the public. She and the Royal Librarian have consulted on what might be of particular interest to her guests and each is given the opportunity of seeing something unique. Actors and playwrights might be shown some of the early scripts that were rejected when the Lord Chamberlain was still the Official Censor. Historians could lose themselves in the ancient documents stored in the Royal Archives, while politicians – and no member of a current government is ever invited to Dine and Sleep – are sometimes shown correspondence between prime ministers and Sovereign of a hundred years ago.

The evening ends with a final drink in the drawing room where The Queen and the Duke of Edinburgh say farewell to their guests. They will not see them the following morning when they leave after breakfast. The valet and housemaid will have washed and ironed anything that requires it and then packed the suitcases, with every garment being protected by a layer of tissue paper to avoid creasing. It is little touches like this that demonstrate the perfection of life among the Royal Family. They take it for granted; for most people, it is the experience of a lifetime.

The Master of the Household insists that tipping is neither expected nor desired, but few guests depart without leaving a discreet £20 note on the mantelpiece. It's a small price to pay for the best food and wine that money can buy – and the entertainment has been priceless.

Every guest writes to The Queen on the day following the Dine and Sleep, to thank her for her hospitality. She reads every letter and they are kept in the Royal Archives for ever. Her Majesty realises the letters have been written out of a sense of duty but she appreciates the sentiments expressed and some of the letters contain little gems of literate and amusing gratitude.

Some guests ask for further information about the treasures they may have been shown during The Queen's personally guided tour, others may seek a copy of the menu – or even the recipe. All are answered, usually by one of the ladies-in-waiting, who have yet to be found wanting in any of the requests. The funniest letters are retained by the ladies in a file named the 'Rogue's Gallery'. Some ask for compensation for damage allegedly caused during their visit. One gentleman said his trousers had been burnt by a footman carelessly smoking a cigarette. Another claimed a dinner jacket had been ruined when he sat on one of Her Majesty's antique dining chairs, while a third said the colour in her dress had run through being badly packed by a housemaid. None of these claims was upheld and no one received any recompense, and none of those particular guests was ever invited again.

If The Queen has been a guest in a private home, she will always write a thank-you letter in her own hand – and she addresses the envelope as well. Perfect manners are second nature to her, and whether she is hostess or guest, she believes the same principles apply.

Being the nation's hostess is not cheap. In 2004 The Queen spent £400,000 on hospitality, apart from the Garden Parties, and a further £400,000 to replenish the Royal Cellars with wines and spirits. This last amount is a good investment as hundreds of bottles are laid down in stock to allow them to age – and to appreciate in value.

The Queen likes to entertain, even if some of the functions are more enjoyable than others. She also likes her guests to enjoy themselves and if that means putting on a show for them, she is perfectly willing to do so – and no one does it better. The Queen, more than most, has a sense of occasion.

three
Wife and
Mother

The Queen must be unique in that, Philip apart, she has never 'dated' another man alone in her life. Unlike most other women of her age, she has never been telephoned by a boyfriend and asked out for dinner, or to go to the theatre or the cinema or a dance. Before she was married she enjoyed a social life of sorts, but her parents controlled it strictly, and the rule was, no romantic entanglements. When she went out it was to specially arranged dinner parties or the theatre, with all her escorts approved by the King and Queen. They usually came from 'suitable' families and were often from one of the more fashionable Guards regiments and she was never permitted to be alone with any of them. But even then, there was only one person she cared for. Philip was the man she was determined to marry and even as a teenager she knew her own mind in spite of all efforts to persuade her otherwise.

Since the day he first came to the public's attention, Prince Philip has had a reputation as something of a ladies' man. Being married to The Queen for over fifty years has done nothing to dent that image; indeed, even at the age of 84, he seems to take great pride in being thought attractive to the opposite sex. One of the most effective personal secrets of his attraction is that whoever he is with, man or woman, he never seems to be looking over your shoulder to see if there is someone more important in the room. He has the ability to focus completely on the person he is talking to at the moment, which is, of course, highly flattering, and where young women are concerned, makes them feel they are making a particularly favourable impression.

His wife also appears to gain a sly satisfaction in knowing that a succession of beautiful young women feel they can get their hands on him, when, in reality, she knows he will always return to her. Philip may have had legions of girlfriends, but, in truth, there has never been any hard evidence that he has slept around; no one has come forward to actually claim they have shared his bed, and with fortunes being offered for 'kiss-and-tell' stories these days, even well-brought-up upper-class girls might have been tempted. The Queen, on the other hand, has only ever had eyes for one man, and that is the man she married in 1947. Philip was, and remains, her dream sweetheart. He is the only man for her and always has been.

She was 13 when she first met 19-year-old Philip Mountbatten in the 1930s, and, if Royal legend is to be believed, it was love at first sight – in her case anyway. Elizabeth is a passionate woman who made no secret of her feelings for Philip almost from the start. He, while being equally physical in his feelings towards women, has never been quite as forthcoming with his declarations of love, even towards her. Not that any of the people who know them both have ever doubted his devotion to his wife, it is just that he does not wear his heart on his sleeve as she does.

Philip won the hand of Princess Elizabeth over the objections of King George VI and Queen Elizabeth – and most of the Royal Household. It was the Princess who stood firm in her determination to marry the man she loved and finally her father gave his reluctant permission. Elizabeth was just 18 in 1944 when Philip first suggested to his cousin the King of Greece that he should act as intermediary in his quest to marry the Princess. King George VI was approached but even though he liked Philip, and admired his courage during the Second World War, he would not countenance her marriage – to anyone – in the immediate future. His Majesty knew that with his daughter reaching adulthood, she would be needed to help with an increasing number of Royal duties and he did not want anything interfering with his plans for her.

Eventually, after three years of waiting, he gave his permission for them to marry when she was 21. He could have withheld his consent until she reached the age of 25 as this is the upper age at which the

Royal Marriages Act 1772 applies. But Elizabeth persuaded her father that no matter how long she would have to wait she was going to marry Philip somehow.

When they became engaged they couldn't even go to the jewellers to choose the ring themselves in case the press caught wind of the relationship. So Philip's mother joined in the conspiracy and bought it for them. Though why a jeweller could not be summoned to Buckingham Palace with a selection from which they could make a choice, which is what happened with almost every subsequent Royal engagement, has never been explained.

It was on 10 July 1947 that the engagement was formally announced: 'It is with the greatest pleasure that the King and Queen announce the betrothal of their dearly beloved daughter The Princess Elizabeth to Lieutenant Philip Mountbatten, RN, son of the late Prince Andrew of Greece and Princess Andrew (Princess Alice of Battenberg), to which union the King has gladly given his consent.'

Four months later, on 20 November, Princess Elizabeth and Philip Mountbatten were married in Westminster Abbey before 1,200 guests, of whom only 150 were invited to Buckingham Palace for the wedding breakfast. There was nothing unusual in this; it wasn't because there was still food rationing in postwar austerity Britain, but because that had been the tradition for generations. Even today, Royal wedding guests have to find their own meals and entertainment after the ceremony. The only people invited to the Palace are family, members of other royal families and selected close friends. Philip and his new bride spent their wedding night at Broadlands, the home of Philip's uncle, Lord Mountbatten. They then journeyed to Scotland where they remained for two weeks at Birkhall on the Balmoral estate. This is the house occupied for fifty years by the Queen Mother and more recently used by Prince Charles and his second wife, Camilla, for their honeymoon.

From the moment of their wedding ceremony, the couple have never really been alone. When they walked together in the grounds at Broadlands or the hills above Balmoral, security men always kept them in sight. It must have been very hard to be romantic with someone always near at hand. Because even in those first days, they were accompanied by personal protection officers, Princess Elizabeth's old nursemaid, the formidable

The Duke of Edinburgh is wearing the full dress uniform of an Admiral of the Fleet as he and The Queen pose at Buckingham Palace on the occasion of the celebrations to mark their Silver Wedding Anniversary on 20 November 1972. (Hulton Archive/Getty Images)

Margaret (Bobo) McDonald, several other servants, footmen and, for the first time, Philip had a personal valet. He now has two.

Unlike most husbands, Philip has had to take second place to his wife for over half a century. They only really had five years of what passes for normal married life in the Royal Family. For part of that time Philip was still a serving naval officer and when he was posted to Malta, where they lived in the Villa Guardanangia, they were able to enjoy the existence that other young married couples take for granted. They joined in the life of the wardroom on the island and even sat in the back row of the local cinema holding hands, surely the first, last and only time a future Queen of England would do such a thing. At Royal Navy dances, Philip would monopolise his wife, even curtly refusing to comply when one of his fellow officers tried to break in. And he invariably instructed the orchestra to play her favourite tune: 'The A-Train' by Duke Ellington. Philip bought Elizabeth an old 78 rpm vinyl record of the song which she eventually wore out when they returned to Britain.

Friends who were stationed with the royal couple in Malta said they were the most tactile newly-weds on the island. They couldn't keep their hands off each other and even if the Princess usually managed to conceal her true feelings beneath her natural royal demeanour, there were occasions when they were glimpsed with their arms around each other's waists walking on the beach. In other words, they were a normal, healthy young couple who enjoyed each other in every sense of the word. That they were a loving couple was later demonstrated when it was revealed that their second child, Princess Anne, who was born in August 1950, had been conceived in Malta the previous December.

Prince Philip's salty sense of humour occasionally came to the fore in the early years of their marriage, even sometimes causing his wife to blush. When Princess Elizabeth was congratulated on her wonderful complexion, Philip is said to have commented, 'Yes, and she's like that all over.' They slept in adjoining rooms, as they still do today, in common with most married couples of their generation and class, but according to James McDonald, one of King George VI's valets, he discovered when he entered Philip's bedroom one morning that the newest member of the Royal Family slept naked. It was some years before he could be persuaded to wear pyjamas.

The difficulty with Philip's Malta posting was that it meant they spent too much time apart from their son Charles. Service wives have always had to put up with long separations from their families and being in Malta with her husband meant that Princess Elizabeth missed being at home in England with Charles for his first Christmas, even though she had been with him on the occasion of his first birthday in November 1949. Many years later, Charles revealed to his authorised biographer, Jonathan Dimbleby, that he felt 'emotionally estranged' from his parents and had yearned for the affection they were 'unable or unwilling to offer'. When this point was put to Prince Philip by Gyles Brandreth he was told, 'We did our best.' Anyway, Charles could hardly claim to have been neglected as his maternal grandmother doted on him and he was virtually brought up by two equally besotted nannies, 'Mrs' (the title was honorary) Lightbody and Miss Anderson.

There was nothing unusual in his upbringing as children of his class and generation were rarely seen by their parents until polished and scrubbed before bedtime, this being long before the days of Royals being 'hands-on' mothers and fathers. When Prince Charles's siblings, Anne, Andrew and Edward, heard what their older brother had said about their parents they were very annoyed with him, and told him so in no uncertain terms. The three younger children all claim to have had very happy childhoods and enjoyed – and still enjoy – a wonderful relationship with their mother and father.

Prince Edward, the Earl of Wessex, is the baby of the family and, as the most reserved of The Queen's children, is still treated with enormous

A Royal wedding at St George's Chapel, Windsor for The Queen's youngest child, Prince Edward, Earl of Wessex and his bride Miss Sophie Rhys-Jones. As the happy couple leave for the reception, they are waved off by their relatives including The Queen, Prince Philip, the Princess Royal and her husband Tim Laurence, Peter and Zara Phillips and the Duke of Gloucester. (© Prism Rights Ltd/Photographers International)

indulgence by The Queen. However, there have been occasions when her patience has been tested. In 1986, Edward joined the Royal Marines, against her advice, but thinking it would please his father, the Captain-General. It proved to be a disastrous decision, though well intentioned. Within three months he found the rigorous training too tough and resigned without completing the course. The publicity that accompanied his resignation, with the tabloids calling him a 'wimp' and a 'sissy', was enough to have caused a breakdown in a lesser man. But his decision showed he knew his own mind and was not afraid to face the consequences. Most people thought that Prince Philip would have been furious with his youngest son, but he proved to be surprisingly sympathetic. It was The Queen who was most disappointed and angry, feeling he had let the family down.

The other occasion when she let him have his own way, when it would have been better if she had put her foot down and ordered him to obey her, was in 1987 when he organised a television show called *It's a Royal Knockout*. Prince Andrew and his then wife took part. So too did Princess Anne, who could never refuse her little brother anything. Prince Charles declined and also refused to allow his wife, Diana, to be involved. The entire show was an embarrassment from start to finish. If The Queen was advised by her aides not to allow it, she ignored them. The children are her one blind spot and this ill-advised escapade, even though it was for charity, was tacky and ridiculous.

Both The Queen and Prince Philip share a great affection for their children and grandchildren, despite stories that abound about Prince Philip being very disappointed in Prince Charles and the way he has behaved in the past. It is true they have had serious disagreements, mainly because Philip wanted his eldest son to be more like him: decisive, confrontational and aggressive. Whereas Charles is acknowledged to be the most indecisive member of the family, who rarely makes up his mind about any issue without changing it several times. It is said that Prince Charles nearly always reflects the opinions of the last person he has spoken to; Prince Philip never changes his mind, he knows exactly what he wants, what he thinks and what he wants everyone else to think. Older members of the Royal Household say they can remember only one occasion when Prince Charles stood up to his father and that was many years ago when they were having a fierce argument and Charles finally shouted at his father 'Remember who you are speaking to – a future King.'

When Princess Anne gave birth to her son Peter, he was the first grandchild of a Sovereign to be born without a title in over 500 years. It was the wish of the Princess and her then husband, Captain Mark Phillips, and The Queen agreed. This was the first official photograph of the infant, taken when he was just 37 days old, with a proud grandmother looking on. (Ron Bell/PA/EMPICS)

Princess Anne, the Princess Royal is the child who has given the most support to her parents. Apart from the single occasion when she and her first husband, Mark Phillips, were divorced and she remarried one of her mother's servants, Tim Laurence, there has never been the slightest cause for concern. In Anne's eyes, her parents, particularly her father, can do no wrong and when Michael Fagan broke into The Queen's bedroom in 1982, thereby causing the biggest upset in Palace security ever known, it was to Anne that The Queen turned for comfort and support.

The present author witnessed an example of the perfect manners displayed by one of The Queen's children during a visit to Gatcombe Park, the home of the Princess Royal. Her butler entered the sitting room and told the Princess, 'Your mother, Her Majesty, is on the telephone Ma'am.' Princess Anne picked up the phone and quite unselfconsciously stood throughout the conversation with her mother. When The Queen said goodbye, the Princess sat down again. It seemed to me that she was completely unaware that what she had done was unusual, but it just showed that an impeccable manner towards their parents is second nature to the Royal children. I once asked the Princess Royal if it was difficult having The Queen as her mother. She replied: 'You've got it the wrong way around. Remember she has been my mother longer than my Queen. I never forget for a moment that she is The Queen, of course, but I can never think of her in any other way than as my mother.'

Prince Andrew, the Duke of York, is the playboy of the family and the one all the others love, even if some of his escapades have caused Royal eyebrows to be raised on occasion. The Queen revealed her opinion of him when she was on a visit to President George Bush in Washington DC. As the President and Mrs Bush accompanied Her Majesty in an elevator to the private quarters in the White House, they chatted amiably and when the elevator doors opened they were greeted by a very young George W. Bush, bare-chested and wearing cowboy boots. As the President apologised, The Queen turned to him and said: 'Don't worry, we have one just like him at home.'

Of course, the fact that Prince Andrew saw active service flying helicopters in the Royal Navy during the Falklands Campaign of 1982, and flew with great distinction, sets him apart from his brothers and is a source of enormous pride to his parents.

The relationship between The Queen and her children is affectionate without being demonstrative and there is a degree of formality that

Another Royal christening, with four generations of Royalty present as Prince William of Wales was christened at Buckingham Palace on 4 August 1982. The baby is held by his mother, the late Diana, Princess of Wales, with his grandmother, The Queen and his great-grandmother, Queen Elizabeth the Queen Mother on either side, as proud godparents stand behind. (Ron Bell/PA/EMPICS)

appears to be a throwback to Victorian times. If The Queen knows one of her children is in the Palace during the afternoon, she will often invite them to join her for tea. But this is not a spur of the moment, spontaneous gesture. Her Majesty's Page will be despatched to enquire if the particular son – or daughter – would care to join their mother. There is rarely a refusal, as The Queen has already been given the daily programme of all her family's movements. But if, for example, the Duke of York is the one who is invited and he is wearing casual clothes, he will always change into something more suitable for tea with The Queen. And when they are announced into her presence, the protocol is always observed: a short, neck bow or curtsy followed by a kiss on the hand and cheek. It never varies and those who have seen it at close hand find it very endearing.

Philip has always claimed that he does not have a jealous bone in his body, a claim many of his friends and relations would challenge having seen him with Elizabeth. No one, man or woman, is permitted to get too close, and he is as jealous of her female friends as he is of any men she knows. Not that he has any reason to be. The Queen has never for one moment given him the slightest reason to question her love and devotion. She is strictly a one-man woman, and she has never wavered in her loyalty to the man she married.

In the early days of their marriage, Philip encountered many difficulties that could have put the relationship under enormous strain. He was forced to take a back seat to his wife, something any new husband would find humiliating if not impossible. And when Princess Elizabeth became Queen in 1952, the situation became even worse as he had to cope with a Royal Household that, in the main, was opposed to him and treated him with disdain bordering on contempt. As a naval officer with no fortune of his own and being a member of the Greek royal family, who were considered to be in the lower ranks of European royalty, many people in Britain, the aristocracy, leading politicians as well as the bulk of the 'old guard' of the Household, considered he was a very lucky man to have been allowed to join the House of Windsor.

Of course, Philip could have pointed out that he was perfectly eligible to be the consort of the then Heiress Presumptive. After all, he too was the great-great-grandson of Queen Victoria, and his own father had been Aide-de-Camp to her, as well as to Edward VII and George V. So he wasn't exactly unused to the ways of British royalty, a point he made dryly to a courtier who attempted to tell him something of the history of Windsor Castle, to which he replied that he didn't need any lessons as his mother had been born there.

However, Philip was not the sort of man to take things lying down. He quickly realised the strength of his own position and rapidly began to assert himself. His Uncle Dickie, Earl Mountbatten of Burma, advised him accordingly, saying, 'Just remember, no matter how important they think they are, they are only servants. You are family.' It was advice he never forgot. Neither did he ever forgive those who had slighted him.

Even if he had to subsume his feelings regarding his role vis-à-vis the British monarchy, there was never any doubt who was the head of the family at home. Elizabeth deferred to her husband in all things connected with family business. It was he who decided where Charles and Anne – and later Andrew and Edward – would be educated. Of course, The Queen had never been to school so she relied on Philip's guidance in this matter. But even when the Queen Mother tried to interfere and have Charles sent to Eton, The Queen backed Philip who insisted that his son should attend Gordonstoun, where he had been such a happy pupil before the war. He went there briefly in 1934, after Kurt Hahn, the school's founder, moved his establishment from Germany. The fact that Charles hated the place from the day he first set foot on its premises didn't make one iota of difference to Philip's decision. And even though The Queen privately sympathised with Charles, she said nothing.

Watching The Queen and Prince Philip together, it soon becomes obvious that they work brilliantly as a team: he is the man forever deliberately challenging, to provoke a reaction, she is more passive, knowing that she doesn't have to say anything even remotely interesting, as she is the reason everyone is there. She is the event itself. They understand each other's moods and complement each other to perfection.

The affection between them is clear for all to see. At receptions in the Palace or Windsor Castle, or when they make their annual visit to the theatre together to see the Royal Variety Show (in aid of charity, not because they enjoy the occasion), he is ever solicitous and can be heard calling his wife 'Dear' while she is often observed placing a hand on his arm, even though she rarely calls him anything but Philip. No member of the Royal Household, or any of their closest friends, can recall hearing the words 'Dear' or 'Darling' passing The Queen's lips. It's not her style. She does not show affection in public, even to her own family. Apart from the time they spent together in Malta, the only occasion when anyone can recall seeing them holding hands was on their wedding day as they came down the Grand Staircase at Buckingham Palace on their way to start their honeymoon. Philip is a tactile man; The Queen is not a naturally tactile woman.

Their marriage has been a brilliant success in spite of the fact that they are not a bit alike in character. He is adventuresome, moody and, contrary to his public image and reputation for making 'gaffes' that outrage many people, highly intellectual. The Queen, on the other hand, could never be described as intellectual or academic. She is cautious to a degree and does not suffer extreme mood swings. He is unpredictable; she is totally predictable. The Queen is non-judgemental about most people; Prince Philip judges everybody. She looks for the best in the men and women she meets; Philip is more pessimistic and suspicious. He needs to be convinced that someone is to be trusted.

One of the things Prince Philip most admires about his wife is her honesty. Unlike nearly every previous monarch, including her own father and grandfather, she does not have a devious bone in her body. She is essentially an honest woman. Her grandfather, George V, refused to allow his cousin, Czar Nicholas II, and his family to have sanctuary in Britain at the time of the Bolshevik revolution, because he was advised it might jeopardise his own position, while The Queen's father, George VI, at first supported the appeaser Lord Halifax in the years leading up to the Second World War, before transferring his allegiance to Winston Churchill, who had never wavered in his hatred of the Nazis, during the conflict.

Philip and Elizabeth have lived their entire married life in the public eye. From the moment of their engagement to the present day, everything they do and say is placed under the microscope of intense scrutiny. When they were first married and he was still a serving naval officer, they spent most of the working week apart. Even when he was posted to a desk job in London and later Greenwich, he spent several days a week – and nights – away from Clarence House. This, in turn, gave rise to speculation that there were problems in the relationship, rumours that have surfaced many times over the years.

Marriage has changed The Queen hardly at all. Certainly as far as her lifestyle is concerned, there has been no difference. She had grown up being surrounded by servants ready and willing to be at her beck and call; she still is. For Philip, the changes caused by his marriage to the woman who was to become his Sovereign, were dramatic. He had never possessed a home of his own – he still doesn't. He had no say in where they would live; his father-in-law, King George VI, decided it initially, advised by his senior courtiers. Then, when the King died in 1952 and Philip and the new Queen were required to move across the road into Buckingham Palace, there was no question of not going. Similarly, weekends at Windsor, Christmas at Sandringham and summers at Balmoral, all take place in homes belonging to his wife. Philip owns nothing. Not many husbands have to suffer this sort of humiliation and subjugate their natural inclinations as family breadwinner. So, if The Queen, in marrying the man she loved, saw virtually no change in her way of life, Philip was the one who made all the sacrifices. After being mentioned in despatches for gallantry during the Second World War, he could have continued in the Royal Navy and enjoyed a brilliant career. He now holds the rank of Admiral of the Fleet, the highest rank in the Royal Navy, but he retired from the active list as a Commander, so obviously, his subsequent promotions came about because of who he is married to, something that gives him no satisfaction whatever.

Shortly before the wedding, on 11 November 1947 the King inducted his elder daughter into the Order of the Garter. He also gave the honour to Philip, but in order to preserve her seniority – some said to remind him to keep his place – His Majesty made sure that Philip did not get his award until a week later, on 19 November. A small thing in itself perhaps, but another slight. The Installation took place the following June on the 600th anniversary of the founding of the Order and was the first Garter ceremony since the end of the Second World War.

The King also refused to make Philip a Prince of the United Kingdom – he had already renounced his Greek title – and it wasn't until ten years later, when The Queen had been on the throne for five years, that she granted him the title of Prince. Of course, Philip had been born a prince, just as The Queen was born a princess, so in that way they are similar to each other – and vastly different from the rest of us.

Philip also gave up the religion he had been baptised into, the Greek Orthodox Church, and in February 1947, became a naturalised British subject. This was a totally unnecessary move as he was a direct descendant of the Electress Sophia of Hanover (mother of George I) and as such, under the Act of Settlement of 1701, he had automatically been British from the day he was born. But in order for Philip to marry the woman who would one day be Queen, every 't' was crossed and 'i' dotted, several times over. Even so, the King's private secretary said of Philip before he was married that he was 'rough, uneducated and would probably be unfaithful'. For an 'uneducated' man, he has proved remarkably adept at mastering the most complicated briefs during his more than half a century of public duties.

He takes his responsibilities very seriously and loves the intricate details of the arrangements made on his behalf. His staff know that they leave out anything at their peril. Philip is not a patient man and with his mercurial mind, added to the fact that he has been in the job longer than any of his Household, he expects rather more from his staff than any other member of the Royal Family. Yet, in spite of his reputation for impatience, they are arguably the most loyal in the entire Royal Household. Most of them would die for him; they tend to stay longer than those working for any other member of the family and Prince Philip defends them strenuously if he feels they have been wrongly accused. This doesn't prevent him from shouting at them at the top of his voice, but they know he doesn't sulk. Once the row is over, it is forgotten.

One of the things The Queen and Prince Philip have in common is their affinity with servicemen and women. They both feel completely at ease with people who have served in the armed forces, particularly if they are old enough to have seen active service during the Second World War. As both Elizabeth and Philip joined up, albeit in The Queen's (then Princess Elizabeth) case for only the final few weeks of the conflict, they feel a natural sympathy with anyone who has been through those dark years. In addition to the rank of Admiral of the Fleet in the Royal Navy Philip holds many other honorary appointments in the Army, Royal Marines and Royal Air Force. He also gained his 'wings' as an RAF pilot and frequently took the controls when flying in one of the aircraft of what was then known as The Queen's Flight (now No. 32 Squadron, The Royal Flight).

As a loving husband, Prince Philip is ultra-protective of his wife. He realises she cannot answer back when there is criticism of either herself or the monarchy, so he speaks up on her behalf. In doing so for over half a century, he has earned a reputation as being rude, outspoken and overbearing. All of which may well be true, but he only speaks on issues that are of deep concern to him and to The Queen. The words he utters very probably mirror opinions of his wife which she is unable to say herself. Even when they are on an engagement together, it is Philip who carries the conversation. As her former Foreign Secretary, David (now Lord) Owen, said, 'Her Majesty doesn't mind in the least appearing to be boring. It doesn't mean she is a boring person, because she certainly is not. It's just that she doesn't feel she has to keep the conversation going all the time.'

Prince Philip, on the other hand, loves to initiate long involved conversations and if they provoke argument so much the better. Some people are afraid to disagree with him, thinking it is not done, but his cousin, Lady Mountbatten, says he welcomes disagreements and loves the hurly burly of a good robust argument. The more people stand up to him, the more he likes it. In fact, the only people who must never answer back are members of the Royal Household. He won't tolerate insubordination at any level and even The Queen's Private Secretary has had to stand quietly and take a torrent of verbal abuse, knowing that if he complains to The Queen, she will invariably back her husband.

As they enter the second half-century of their life together, The Queen and Prince Philip are thoroughly enjoying their twilight years together. They both look years younger than they are. The Queen still rides at Windsor and Sandringham while Philip remains a frequent user of the Buckingham Palace swimming pool. Hence his athletic and still trim figure.

One way in which their relationship has altered over the years since they married in 1947 is that in those early days, Philip tended to overcompensate in his efforts to be seen as head of the family. He would deliberately tell The Queen to shut up when he disagreed with something she had said and, it is said, even called her a bloody fool on more than one occasion. In turn, she was much gentler, rarely fighting back. Today, he has become more solicitous towards her, never saying anything that would hurt her and she has become more assertive, often telling him to be quiet when he has overstepped the mark. He quite likes the subtle change in his wife, often giving a gentle smile when she answers back. It's as if they are sharing a private joke.

Elizabeth and Philip have always had a great sense of the ridiculous. He says that sometimes it is the only thing that keeps them sane. If they didn't laugh privately at some of the antics they are forced to witness with outward solemnity, they would cry.

In 2002 The Queen suffered two great losses when both her younger sister, Princess Margaret, and her beloved mother, Queen Elizabeth, died within weeks of each other. It meant that this devoted daughter and sister was now the sole survivor of the original 'Firm' as her father, King George VI, liked to call the four members of the family. Nobody saw her shed a tear in public, though her grief was evident at both funerals. There was only one person she could turn to for comfort in the privacy of their home and that was Philip, the man who had supported her for over fifty years. He knew she needed to grieve and he didn't interfere. But he was there when she needed him, offering whatever sympathy he felt she wanted. Philip is in a unique position; he is the only person in the world who could do so, and while he is not sentimental – and The Queen would not wish him to be – he is what she once called him, 'my rock' – a phrase she used long before the late Diana, Princess of Wales was said to have used it in describing her one-time butler.

Prince Philip is exactly the right sort of man to be husband and consort to The Queen. She needs someone to whom she can confide her fears and hopes, knowing that there will never be the slightest chance her innermost secrets will be revealed. If Philip were to write a true account of his life with Elizabeth: the trials and tribulations, the disappointments they have suffered because of their children's behaviour, the way they have survived severe criticism – particularly after the untimely death of the late Diana, Princess of Wales – and the way in which attitudes to the monarchy have changed during the years they have been married, it would be one of the most explosive books ever written. Of course, he will never do it. But he has been religious in keeping a diary, which will be stored away from prying eyes in the Royal Archives hidden in the Round Tower at Windsor Castle. Perhaps in a hundred years all will be revealed. By that time it will be Prince William's grandchildren or great-grandchildren who will be the custodians of royal secrets – and maybe no one will still be interested by then.

One thing is certain today. Philip and Elizabeth's is a partnership of two people who not only love each other, but are also one another's best friend. Together with their children they give the impression that they neither need nor want anyone else.

Happy the *Bride?*

T here are few things in the world that fire the imagination of the British people more than a Royal wedding. It is a red-letter day in the national calendar and an occasion for general congratulation and celebration.

All this was brought sharply into focus once more in April 2005 when the Prince of Wales announced he was to marry Camilla Parker Bowles, his companion of many years.

At any wedding, attention naturally focuses on the bride, but when the bridegroom is expected to be the next King, there is an extra sense of anticipation and excitement. Which made the initial indifference and, in some cases, outright hostility that greeted the nuptials of Prince Charles and Camilla Parker Bowles all the more marked. In addition, Camilla, now Her Royal Highness the Duchess of Cornwall, became overnight one of the most important women in the country, though when The Queen issued the official Order of Precedence at Court, shortly after the wedding, it was seen that the Duchess was placed in fourth place, behind the Princess Royal and Princess Alexandra. When Lady Diana Spencer married the Prince of Wales in 1981, she was preceded by only The Queen and the Queen Mother.

Prince Charles was required by a 233-year-old law to seek the permission of his mother before proposing to Camilla – surely the only 56-year-old man this century to have to undergo this humiliating ordeal. Under the Royal Marriages Act, 1772, all lineal descendants of George II are bound to obtain the consent of the Sovereign before marrying. The Act was brought into being at the insistence of George III, who brought pressure to bear on Parliament when he discovered that his younger brother, the Duke of Cumberland, had made an 'unsuitable' secret marriage to Lady Anne Horton, the disreputable widow of a commoner.

The interview between The Queen and her eldest son was conducted in her sitting room at Buckingham Palace and was entirely formal. There was nothing of the cosy mother and son chat one might have expected. It was the heir to the throne seeking the permission of the Sovereign to marry.

Of course, as we now know, The Queen gave her consent, but, according to a senior courtier, as a mother, she is believed to have had serious doubts about the wisdom of her eldest son's choice of bride, knowing that her soon-to-be daughter-in-law was still regarded by millions of people throughout the world as the most hated and vilified woman in Britain since the Duke of Windsor's wife, Wallis Simpson, in 1936. Camilla will forever be remembered as the cause of the break-up of Prince Charles's first marriage, and blamed by some, as the indirect cause of Diana's death.

If The Queen had withheld her consent, Prince Charles – as he is clearly over the age of 25, the upper age at which the Act applies to members of the Royal Family – could have signified to Parliament, through the Privy Council, his intention to marry Camilla, and unless both the House of Commons and the House of Lords expressed their formal disapproval within twelve months, the marriage would be lawful.

The only previous occasion when The Queen found herself in the position where she might have had to withhold her consent to a Royal marriage was in the 1950s, when her sister, Princess Margaret, was considering marriage to a divorced man, Group Captain Peter Townsend. As Supreme Governor of the Church of England, it would have been almost impossible for The Queen to give her permission in those days, but she did not have to make this difficult decision as Princess Margaret decided not to marry Townsend. The Prime Minister of the day, Sir Winston Churchill, later indicated that if he had been asked formally he would have been unable to 'advise' Her Majesty that the marriage could take place. However, recently released official papers suggest that the government of the day had considered the possibility of the marriage and did not believe it to be impossible.

Of course attitudes towards marriage and divorce have changed considerably during The Queen's reign but a large proportion of the population still believes that a Royal marriage should be a conventional affair and not the source of controversy.

There could not be a greater contrast between the low-key civil ceremony that took place in the Guildhall in Windsor on Saturday 9 April 2005 and the pageantry and splendour of the wedding of the Prince of Wales and Lady Diana Spencer at St Paul's Cathedral on 29 July 1981, barely a month after the bride's twentieth birthday. Then it was a day of joy for everyone involved: an occasion that was a combination of deep emotion,

The Queen and Prince Philip did not attend the civil wedding service of Prince Charles and Mrs Camilla Parker Bowles on 9 April 2005, but they did join the couple for the official photographs in the White Drawing Room at Windsor Castle. Also in the picture is the bride's father, Major Bruce Shand (seated) with, from left to right standing: Prince Harry, Prince William, and Tom and Laura Parker Bowles, the bride's children from her first marriage. (Hugo Bernand/Pool/Getty Images)

formal ceremony and vociferous enthusiasm from the thousands who lined the wedding route and the millions throughout the world watching the event on television.

Diana was everyone's idea of the perfect fairy-tale princess and no one will forget the sight of The Queen dancing a little jig in the forecourt of Buckingham Palace as the couple left on the first stage of their honeymoon.

Conversely, this latest Royal wedding was plagued with problems from the time it was announced that Charles and Camilla were engaged. The difficulties over the venue, the death of Pope John Paul II – which caused a last-minute change of date, a postponement of 24 hours from Friday to Saturday, in itself an unheard of break with royal tradition – the blessing in St George's Chapel, the number of guests being invited to the service and then those going to the chapel and the reception afterwards, even whether or not the marriage could be legally solemnised, all proved to be a massive embarrassment to the Royal Family, with even The Queen embroiled in the controversy. But more importantly, in the view of many respected observers of the Royal scene, the low-key civil wedding service may well have hastened the end of much of the full-blown pageantry that British people have come to associate with Royalty.

When The Queen (as Princess Elizabeth) and Prince Philip married in 1947, it was the first Royal wedding to take place in the aftermath of the Second World War. Britain was still in the grip of postwar austerity with severe rationing of everything from clothes to food. King George VI felt it would be too ostentatious to hold the ceremony at the traditional venue, Westminster Abbey, and he suggested a quiet, private affair in St George's Chapel, Windsor Castle. But the Labour Government persuaded him that the people needed some light relief in their lives, so he relented and allowed the abbey to be used and a full State wedding to take place. It also happened to be excellent public relations for both the government and the Royal Family. Since then, Royal weddings have invariably been great public occasions full of pomp and pageantry.

Royal weddings usually take months, sometimes years to plan. Formal announcements are never made until everyone concerned has agreed every detail. Buckingham Palace has a superb system of 'referring back' when an occasion is in the planning stage. Weddings, funerals, the State Opening of Parliament, Trooping the Colour, all the major events involving

The date was 20 November 1947, and Princess Elizabeth and her husband, Lieutenant Philip Mountbatten, pose for the official wedding pictures following their marriage ceremony in Westminster Abbey. (Topical Press Agency/Getty Images)

The Queen and her family are recorded in minute detail in the files of the Lord Chamberlain, who is in overall charge and who handles the ceremonial side, including sending out the invitations. The Master of the Household is responsible for all domestic arrangements, such as the seating plans, and the Crown Equerry looks after the transport requirements. They all know exactly what they are doing, because they have done it all many times before. Unfortunately, there was no precedent for this particular wedding. It was unique in the history of the Royal Family – and it showed.

The difficulties between Prince Charles's Household based at Clarence House and the Royal Household at Buckingham Palace have been well documented. There are very few areas on which they agree, with the Palace claiming that Prince Charles has set up an 'alternative court' across the road. Events leading up to the wedding revealed the Prince's staff lacked both the experience and understanding of Royal convention needed to manage something as delicate and controversial as the second marriage of the heir to the throne to a divorced woman whose ex-husband is still living, despite the fact that the Prince of Wales's Principal Private Secretary, Sir Michael Peat, had served very successfully as The Queen's Keeper of the Privy Purse for several years. But in that role he did not have to deal with such delicate and personal matters as a Royal wedding. So The Queen ordered her Lord Chamberlain, Lord Luce, to take charge of the arrangements and on the day itself, everything went like clockwork. Some months later, when the dust had settled, it was announced that one of The Queen's most senior and trusted aides, Sir Malcolm Ross, who had been Comptroller of the Lord Chamberlain's Office for over twenty years, had been appointed as Head of the Household of the Prince of Wales and the Duchess of Cornwall. He took over in January 2006 and it was seen as a direct result of the chaos surrounding the earlier disastrous wedding arrangements.

The Archbishop of Canterbury, Dr Rowan Williams, was known to have had severe reservations about the union, even though he agreed, after private consultations with The Queen, to conduct the service of blessing (or dedication) in St George's Chapel following the civil ceremony outside the castle walls. If the Archbishop's expression was anything to go by during the service, it appeared that he had retained his doubts and was merely performing a duty demanded by The Queen of the senior cleric of the Church of England.

But contrary to Palace rumours at the time, Dr Williams was not approached by Prince Charles to see if a church wedding could be arranged. Charles knew that would be a non-starter and the Archbishop would be bound to refuse, so he spared him that particular embarrassment. But Prince Charles did have a private audience with the Archbishop in the weeks leading to the ceremony and persuaded His Grace to allow a Windsor blessing in spite of his obvious misgivings. The Archbishop was adamant that the service in St George's Chapel should be one of repentance on the part of bride and bridegroom, not a glorification of the marriage, which is why on the day itself, he refused to wear his full State robes and appeared instead in the simplest vestments he possessed, with the full agreement of The Queen.

Royal protocol demanded that The Queen and the Duke of Edinburgh did not attend the actual wedding service, though they were present at the blessing and at the reception, which Her Majesty paid for, as she did for all her children's weddings, including Princess Anne's second marriage to Tim Laurence, which was held in Scotland. Indeed, if Prince Charles and

Mrs Parker Bowles had opted for a wedding at Crathie Parish Church, just outside the gates of Balmoral Castle, as Anne did, most of the uncertainties surrounding this affair could have been avoided. The Church of Scotland has a more relaxed and tolerant view towards marrying divorced couples than the Church of England. And, of course, The Queen would have been spared any awkwardness, as she is not Supreme Governor of the Church of Scotland, so there would have been no conflict. However, members of Her Majesty's Ecclesiastical Household in Scotland were believed to be against holding the service north of the border anyway, because Scotland might then be accused of allowing itself to be used as a convenience by the heir to the throne.

The mechanics of a Royal wedding and all the arrangements are the responsibility of the Royal Household, subject to approval by The Queen, who inspects every detail from the size of the lettering on the invitations, to which of her dinner services is to be used. Everything is worked out with split-second precision. When Lady Diana Spencer was due to leave Clarence House for St Paul's Cathedral, she wanted to exercise the bride's prerogative and arrive 2 minutes late. The then Crown Equerry, Sir John Miller, was horrified as he had rehearsed the route several times, stopwatch in hand. They reached a compromise by allowing her to arrive at the cathedral steps just 30 seconds after the appointed time, but he was not best pleased.

At previous Royal weddings, the majority of the gold-edged invitations were sent to 'must-have' guests: other European royalty, political leaders and close friends of The Queen; the bride's family have very little say in who is to be invited. This was the case when the Prince and Princess of Wales were married, again for the Duke and Duchess of York and when Prince Edward married Sophie Rhys-Jones in St George's Chapel (the only one of The Queen's children not to have a full-blown State wedding ceremony in Westminster Abbey or St Paul's Cathedral). So, Camilla's father, Major Bruce Shand, had nothing to do except turn up, and as it was a civil ceremony, he didn't even have to give his daughter away.

Those guests who were invited to the blessing in St George's Chapel received tickets, each one numbered and where they were to be seated indicated by the colour of the ticket: red for Royalty, blue for VIP guests and white for everyone else. So Tony and Cherie Blair found themselves near the front while the gardeners at Highgrove, who were delighted and surprised to be included on the guest list, sat at the back of the church. It's the way the Royal machinery works.

There was no horse-drawn State coach with liveried attendants for the bride and groom's short journey from Windsor's Guildhall to the castle. The Queen had decided, it must be said with Prince Charles's approval, that they should be driven in one of the Royal cars. The guests who needed transport found themselves seated in a fleet of minibuses – as they were at Prince Edward's wedding. It was all very low-key and democratic. But the end result was a great success and St George's Chapel looked magnificent, particularly the branches of white blossom, chosen by Prince Charles, that decorated the inside.

Unfortunately with Royal weddings, the couple being married seem to have very little to do with the affair. The bride did choose her own outfit; nearly everyone said she looked radiant, but that apart, The Queen assumed responsibility for all the arrangements. Charles and Camilla didn't even get to select the music to be played at the reception by musicians from one of Her Majesty's regiments; she did that. Neither did they have any say in what the guests ate and drank. The Queen chose a cold finger buffet for Prince Charles and his bride, consisting of fresh salmon, chicken, tiny lamb cutlets and salad; the Yeoman of the Royal Cellars selected, again with The Queen's approval, the wine and champagne to accompany the meal.

The only occasion when the bride and groom did take over the entire show was when Charles and Diana married. Then it was nearly all Prince Charles's decisions, he became the impresario, choosing St Paul's Cathedral because he wanted more guests (2,500) than could be accommodated in Westminster Abbey (1,200), and he wanted three orchestras to play, a famous choir to sing and the New Zealand soprano Dame Kiri te Kanawa to perform. It wasn't quite what The Queen would have arranged but on this one occasion she gave in and allowed her son to have the extravaganza he wanted.

The Queen and Prince Philip received 1,347 wedding presents when they married, many of which are still stored in a heated building in Windsor Great Park, as homes cannot be found for them in any of the Royal residences. No doubt a similar fate awaits many of the gifts their eldest son will have received on the occasions of both his marriages, as Camilla has removed nearly all traces of Diana from Highgrove, the Gloucestershire home they once shared and of which she is now the mistress.

Although The Queen is said to have disapproved of Camilla as a prospective daughter-in-law, within weeks of the wedding, she showed she had welcomed the former Mrs Parker Bowles into the family by including her at several important ceremonial functions such as the sixtieth anniversary services of the end of the Second World War and the Trooping the Colour Parade, when Camilla was invited for the first time onto the balcony of Buckingham Palace to watch the traditional flypast, and in July 2005, she and Prince Charles joined The Queen and Prince Philip at an Afternoon Garden Party. The Queen also ordered that flags should be flown on public buildings on the occasion of Camilla's birthday.

Clarence House announced, when news of the engagement was released, that Camilla would be known as the Duchess of Cornwall, not the Princess of Wales, which, as the wife of the Prince of Wales, she is legally anyway. But it is obvious to seasoned observers of the Royal scene that, again with The Queen's approval, she is being groomed for her eventual role as Queen. Elizabeth II is above all a realist and pragmatist who believes that as the years go by – and assuming Her Majesty's anticipated longevity – much of the antagonism towards Camilla will disappear and she will be accepted not only as the wife – but also as Queen Consort – of Charles when he becomes King. So far as The Queen is concerned, the continuity of the monarchy in Britain is the most important accomplishment, and if that means Charles and Camilla on the throne, so be it. Anyway, she won't be around to witness it.

Highland
Holidays

I f anyone suggested to The Queen that she might like to spend a month lying on a beach sunbathing in the Bahamas, she would be both horrified and mystified. Horrified because the very idea of a vacation doing nothing is abhorrent to her and mystified that anyone would even have the temerity to imagine that such an outrageous idea would have the slightest appeal.

One of her ladies-in-waiting once told her that she had been abroad on holiday, to Barbados, and the trip had cost her £5,000. Her Majesty couldn't believe that anyone would spend such an amount on what to her seemed a frivolous and pretty dreadful holiday. Unlike her sister, the late Princess Margaret, who was a self-confessed sun-worshipper, The Queen has never once had a beach holiday. She doesn't care for hot weather, constant sunshine or balmy climates. Even when she and Prince Philip lived in Malta during his Royal Navy posting to the island, she rarely spent her afternoons sunbathing like most of the other wives, though she did enjoy swimming in the Mediterranean.

She has always claimed that her idea of the perfect break is several weeks in the Highlands of Scotland – her spiritual home – staying at Balmoral Castle. The weather simply doesn't come into it; it's nearly always raining anyway, with heavy mountain mist, and, as sunbathing is the last thing on her mind, she enjoys wrapping up in warm clothes with a headscarf and wellington boots, and walking for miles across the heather-strewn hills surrounding the castle. Balmoral has been passed down from Sovereign to Sovereign since it was purchased by Queen Victoria, so The Queen has been going there since she was a child, when she and Princess Margaret spent part of every summer with their parents in the Highlands.

As mistress of Balmoral, The Queen likes nothing more than the traditional holidays that originated with her great-great-grandmother 150 years ago. It was Prince Albert who bought the castle privately from the Earl of Fife for £31,500 in 1852 and spent the next three years together with his architect William Smith practically rebuilding it from scratch.

Today the castle plays roughly the same part in the life of the Sovereign in Scotland as her other privately owned residence, Sandringham, does in England. In other words, while Buckingham Palace and Windsor Castle are the official ceremonial residences in England and the Palace of Holyroodhouse occupies the same position in Scotland, Sandringham and Balmoral are the homes where The Queen and her family spend their holidays and where they can relax in private. The castle is approached via a long winding, country road from Ballater, the nearest town, and there are magnificent lawns surrounding the house, a beautiful rose garden – and a golf course, whose most frequent user is Prince Andrew, the Duke of York.

The outside of Balmoral gives the impression of a forbidding and pretentious gaunt and granite country house masquerading as a genuine Scottish baronial castle, and the interior also ensures that the Scottish style of Queen Victoria's time is preserved. There is still a mass of heavy Victorian furniture and dark wallpaper. The rooms are comfortable if a little intimidating and there is no doubt that the original, and subsequent, royal lairds have gone out of their way to make it clear that this is a royal Scottish home. Tartan is in evidence in every room, with the drawing room boasting its famous 'Balmoral' tartan carpet. Harold Wilson said the place was a 'time warp' where nothing seemed to have changed in over a century and where there was an air of 'Brigadoon', the romantic Scottish village immortalised in a Hollywood film where everyone dressed in Highland kilts and tartans, but which wasn't a real place at all.

When The Queen moves to Balmoral for the summer, the Court goes with her. The logistics are incredible, with horses and dogs to be transported in fleets of vans, lorries and horseboxes. Then there is the question of The Queen and Prince Philip's entertainment. Weeks before the annual migration, the Master of the Household contacts Paul Whybrew, The Queen's page, and asks him to find out what Her Majesty would like to see, on television or in the private cinema. He then obtains copies from the BBC and ITV and from film companies and these are packed to be transported north. Angela Kelly, The Queen's personal assistant, is a valuable source of information on both The Queen's and Prince Philip's current favourites. She also might mention one or two dozen books they want to read and these are obtained (they rarely have to buy any of them as the suppliers are only too pleased to give them free). The rule with books is that they must be brand new hardbacks as the Royals will not read paperbacks, and unopened as they like to be the first to handle them.

When the Royal Family holidays at Balmoral they attend many of the local events. On this occasion, some 3,000 guests joined The Queen on the lawn of Balmoral Castle to watch the Highland Band of the Scottish Division Beating Retreat. Alongside Her Majesty is the Lord Lieutenant of Aberdeenshire, Captain C. Farquharson, with his deputy Mr W. Ferguson. (David Cheskin/PA/EMPICS)

One of the ways in which The Queen relaxes at Balmoral is by 'bat-catching'. She and one of her footmen spend part of almost every afternoon wielding large butterfly nets with which they attempt to catch the bats that hang from the upper reaches of the ballroom and hall. They then release them into the open, only for the bats to return at night – and The Queen carries out exactly the same operation the following day. The fact that she achieves nothing with this exercise doesn't deter her; she's been doing it ever since she first came to the castle as a young princess and she will probably carry on until she drops.

A main attraction of Balmoral for the Royal Family is that the people of Ballater, and the surrounding areas, are so used to seeing Royalty that they leave them alone. There is no fuss when one of the family appears in the local shops and the local people jealously guard the privacy they know the Royals desire when they are on holiday.

Queen Victoria may have loved Balmoral and this part of Scotland but when she was in residence she was seen in public only on rare occasions, and then accompanied by the retinue that escorted her everywhere, formality being the order of the day. Edward VII also enjoyed his holidays in the Highlands, but he, too, although he relaxed the routine slightly, never patronised local businesses in person. It was The Queen's father, King George VI, and his Consort, Queen Elizabeth, who really paved the way for the Royal Family to become accepted into the locality as 'one of us'.

When the young princesses, Elizabeth and Margaret, accompanied their parents to Balmoral they were often seen shopping in Ballater where they became familiar figures to the local tradesmen. Of course, these were the days before security demands meant that no member of the family could venture forth without being escorted by an armed bodyguard. Today, even a simple shopping excursion into Ballater involves a 'recce' trip by a member of the Royalty Protection Department to make sure it is safe for his principal to enter the premises they wish to visit. The locals realise this is a necessary precaution and take the intrusion in their stride, because the association with Royalty has been good for business in Ballater, acting as a magnet and putting it on the 'must see' list for tourists from all over the world. Almost every shop boasts a Royal coat-of-arms and a By Appointment sign over its door, and every year thousands of visitors flock to the town, in the hope both of seeing a member of the Royal Family and of buying a souvenir from one of the 'Royal' shops.

As Laird of Balmoral, The Queen takes a special interest in the life of the villages and towns surrounding her estate. She is kept informed of all the local news through her factor, the man who runs Balmoral on a day-to-day basis on her behalf, and she and Prince Philip, who has titular responsibility for the estate, are frequent guests of honour at special functions and sporting events held in the area.

The Braemar Gathering is one of the biggest social and sporting events in the Scottish calendar and The Queen rarely fails to put in an appearance. When the late Diana, Princess of Wales paid her first visit to Balmoral she accompanied The Queen to Braemar and gave the outward appearance of enjoying herself – as a dutiful daughter-in-law – but she later told friends that she found the entire experience both boring and pointless, particularly 'the idea of grown men trying to throw telegraph poles', a reference to the ancient sport of tossing the caber. The Queen was dismayed and disappointed that her daughter-in-law, whom she had

One of the immovable feasts of the summer season in Scotland is the Braemar Games and The Queen and Prince Philip always like to attend when they are able. Throughout their stay in the Highlands, male members of the family wear kilts, with the ladies also sporting tartan dress. [© Tim Graham/CORBIS]

assumed would be enthusiastic about the country pursuits that form the mainstay of the Royal Family's holidays since she had grown up in the country, was, in fact, totally uninterested in riding, shooting and fishing.

Life for The Queen and her family at Balmoral follows as regimented a routine as Royal life anywhere. Her Majesty likes things to be well ordered and she demands to know in advance what the next day – and the day after that – is going to bring. She likes to keep her guests entertained – by that she means busy – so every minute of every day is accounted for, with detailed arrangements and times for breakfast, lunch, afternoon tea and dinner, and the hours in between filled with walks, picnics and, for new guests, tours of the estate. Her Majesty loves to show people the small house she had built for Prince Philip near the river, and en route she will also point out the most famous of the other lodges, that which Queen Victoria built for her favourite ghillie, John Brown. Brown's statue, again erected by Queen Victoria, was removed by King George V from its prominent place in front of Balmoral Castle and placed in the woodland near Loch Muick, the lake where Prince Philip taught his daughter, Anne, to sail.

Life at Balmoral may be dictated by protocol, but there is a lot less formality than at Buckingham Palace, Windsor or even at Sandringham, both for guests and staff. If a special guest is invited to see Prince Philip's lodge, they may have a light snack there and afterwards The Queen has been known to wash the dishes herself with the guest drying. Picnics are a great favourite at Balmoral, but they are not like any most people enjoy. Before the Royal Family arrive at the chosen spot, footmen will have carried there all the paraphernalia required: the food in special hampers (The Queen likes to lay out the sandwiches herself and does not appreciate offers of help), thermos flasks of coffee and tea, and wine and beer – properly chilled of course. Then, once everything has been prepared, they retreat to a safe distance so that Prince Philip can light the barbecue and cook the steaks and sausages.

There was one recent occasion when things did not go quite as planned. His Royal Highness found he did not have any matches to light the fire, nor did any of the footmen. He exploded and ordered one to run all the way back to the castle – a journey of over a mile both ways – to bring him a box of matches. The fact that he had not thought to take any himself simply did not occur to him. Royalty may not always be right, but they are never wrong.

Prince Philip organises the daily programme, which is printed and circulated to the family, guests and household. He hates the thought of not having every waking moment gainfully employed and guests who are not used to his extraordinary energy sometimes find themselves longing for a few quiet minutes to themselves. The programme is helpful to guests and staff, particularly the maids and dressers, as ladies sometimes need to change clothes up to four times a day: breakfast, sporting outfits, afternoon dresses for tea and always long dresses at dinner.

Shooting and fishing are the two main sports associated with Deeside, and the 50,000 or so acres of the Balmoral estate with its miles of heather moors are ideal for stalking stags and other wildlife. Prince Philip likes few things more than spending hours patiently stalking a stag completely unaware of the discomfort so long as he gets his prey in the end. One day he was thwarted just as he lined up a target in his sights. He was about to fire when two young people walked unconcernedly across his eye-line. When he shouted to them, using a few choice expletives, asking what they thought they were doing, even he was lost for words when they replied that they were carrying out tasks for their Duke of Edinburgh Award medals.

The Queen, as Princess Elizabeth, was first taught to shoot when she was 15 and a year later she shot her first stag at Balmoral. For years she enjoyed stalking in the hills, and couldn't understand why some of her female guests didn't share her enthusiasm for lying around in wet clothes for hours on end. The grouse moors on the estate are very productive but inevitably there have been occasions when there were no grouse and The Queen has been known to cancel a house party on the grounds that, if there is no sport, what is the point of people turning up?

During their eight-week stay in Scotland The Queen and Prince Philip like to invite an eclectic mix of guests to join them. The list is usually suggested by the Master of the Household and amended by Her Majesty. Old friends such as Countess Mountbatten (Patricia Mountbatten is Prince Philip's cousin) are regular guests, and Her Majesty's former personal police protection officer, ex-Chief Superintendent James Beaton, who comes from Aberdeen and who has become very friendly with Prince Philip in particular since his retirement, is invited to shoot. It was Beaton who saved Princess Anne's life when an attempt was made to kidnap her just four months after she and Mark Phillips were married. Beaton was shot five times and for his gallantry was awarded the George Cross, the highest award for bravery a civilian can win. The main difference Jim Beaton has found in the attitude of his hosts from when he was working for them, is that in those days he was merely 'Beaton', now, as a guest, he is addressed as 'Jim'.

The River Dee, which flows through part of the Balmoral estate, provides some of the best fishing in Scotland, and the late Queen Mother thought nothing of standing up to her thighs in icy water for hours on end, even in her sixties. When she became a little elderly for active participation in one of her favourite sports, she would sit on the banks watching her grandson, Prince Charles and later, both of her great-grandsons, Princes William and Harry.

The Queen has never been very keen on fishing, neither does she enjoy stalking any longer. But she does love to walk for miles through the grounds, usually on her own, apart from the company of several of her dogs, and always with one of the ever-present protection officers following at a discreet distance. Balmoral is criss-crossed with footpaths and it would be all too easy for someone to infiltrate the woods.

Prince Philip has entered into the spirit of being a true Scottish host with tremendous enthusiasm, but in the early days of their marriage, when King George VI was still alive, he did not fit in quite so easily. For his first visit he had to borrow a dinner jacket from his uncle Dickie, Earl Mountbatten, and Princess Margaret was highly amused to see her brother-in-law wearing a pair of her father's old plus fours. He was also prevailed upon to wear a kilt, as all members of the Royal Family do. But when he turned up at an evening of Scottish dancing and gave an irreverent mock curtsy to the King, His Majesty was definitely not amused.

Today, Prince Philip, and all the other members of the Royal Family, proudly wear the Balmoral tartan, another of Queen Victoria and Prince Albert's inventions. About 1850 they ordered a special tartan in a distinctive red and grey pattern that would be exclusive to the Royal Family. Later, Edward VIII authorised the registration of the sett so that no one else could manufacture it – and make a profit. There is also a Balmoral tweed that all the family, and some privileged members of the Household, wear for shooting and other country sports. The tweed is comparatively recent and was designed for King George VI in 1937 and, again, no member of the public is permitted to wear it.

The one thing any guest at Balmoral can be sure of is that he or she will not go hungry. The estate provides an abundance of fresh salmon, game and venison, and there is always plenty of roast beef on the menu. Added to which are the delights of Scottish baking so most people leave having put on a few pounds.

Wherever The Queen goes, she is never fully off duty, even at Balmoral when Parliament is in recess. Her days invariably include several hours with her Private Secretary working on her 'boxes', the official papers from government departments and Commonwealth countries that she has to attend to immediately. The rest of the family know they have to leave her alone when the courier arrives with the day's despatches and occasionally a meeting of the Privy Council has to be called at the castle when ministers need the Royal Assent for particular pieces of legislation.

Most ministers quite enjoy being summoned to Balmoral. They know they are going to be given superb hospitality and if it is too late for them to return to London or their constituencies at the end of the day, they are offered the chance to enjoy The Queen's holiday home overnight. For those who are seeing the castle for the first time it is a unique experience; the difficulty for some is that they may have come unprepared for the rigours of a Highland summer. More than one minister has turned up wearing lightweight clothes and shoes, only to find their more experienced colleagues have brought heavy tweeds and sensible brogues. One even took the precaution of bringing a pair of thermal 'long johns' to guard against the possibility of a chill. Harold Wilson was once overheard complaining about the lack of heating in the castle; this was in August after all. When his hostess learned of his discomfort she merely remarked that 'he should wear an extra sweater'.

In September, the prime minister of the day and their spouse are invited to spend a weekend with The Queen. This usually means arriving on a Friday afternoon, spending Saturday with the Royal Family, attending the local Crathie Parish Church on Sunday morning and departing after lunch. Crathie Church is another building associated with Queen Victoria, who laid its foundation stone in 1893 and was then present when the church was dedicated two years later. The south transept is the royal transept used only by the Royal Family, the Household and The Queen's guests. The Queen always worships at Crathie when she is at Balmoral and she invites guests to join her but there is no compulsion; she never insists on their attendance.

Prime ministers have appreciated the occasion of their Royal visits in many different ways: Harold Wilson loved the place and thoroughly enjoyed himself every time he and his wife, Mary, stayed. James Callaghan (later Lord Callaghan of Cardiff) felt equally at home, and he and The Queen spent most of the weekends he was there walking in the garden (as they did at Buckingham Palace where he arrived for his weekly Tuesday audience). Alec Douglas Home, who resigned his title as Earl of Home to become Prime Minister, was a fellow landowner with large estates in Scotland, so he was completely at home during his weekend stays at Balmoral. He and The Queen – and the Duke of Edinburgh – would spend hours discussing the relative merits of their fishing and shooting.

Edward Heath was, apparently, never terribly comfortable in Royal company and when anyone near her appears to be nervous, it puts The

Queen slightly on edge, so the atmosphere isn't relaxed. With Margaret Thatcher there was usually an extra degree of formality while the Prime Minister's indifference to the countryside was apparent to everyone. She did not enjoy the outdoor life of the Royals with their complete disregard for the weather, but her husband, Denis, was a wonderful companion and always a welcome guest at all The Queen's homes. Prince Philip and Denis got on well and whenever they were together the jokes flew thick and fast.

The Queen's first Prime Minister, Sir Winston Churchill, invited himself to Balmoral during the first year of her reign. At 78, he was by far the oldest guest – The Queen was only 26 at the time – but he was disgruntled when he was not invited to shoot. Prince Philip thought, rightly, that it would be too much for him as he hadn't held a gun for over twenty years, but Churchill told one of his aides that he could have held his own with any of them. Churchill had visited Balmoral many times during previous reigns, the

earliest being as far back as that of King Edward VII. During the reign of The Queen's grandfather, George V, Churchill held the record of having shot three stags in succession in a single afternoon.

Of all the prime ministers who have served The Queen, the most recent – and the youngest – Tony Blair, gives the appearance of disliking the obligatory visit to Balmoral the most. The official reason for these visits is for the prime

Every American president since Dwight D. Eisenhower, has been a guest of The Queen during their term of office, but only President Ronald Reagan accepted Her Majesty's offer to join her in a morning ride. Of course, as a former star in several Hollywood western films, he was fully at home in the saddle and afterwards said he had never enjoyed an official visit more. (Jayne Fincher/© Photographers International)

minister to brief The Queen personally on any matters on which she may need more information than she has received in the post. And this is also the only time they will meet during the long summer Parliament break, and, indeed, until the weekly audiences start again in October. The Queen goes out of her way to make all her guests comfortable, but the Blairs have tried in the past to curtail the visits, arriving on Saturday and leaving the next day. The Queen, of course, doesn't take this personally, but senior members of the Royal Household, who also take this opportunity to hold important talks with their opposite numbers on the Prime Minister's staff, find it irksome and churlish.

One of The Queen's staff told the present author that the difficulties with the Blairs usually arise because of Cherie's attitude to The Queen and the Royal Family. While she is correct to Her Majesty, she barely conceals her indifference towards some of the younger Royals, with the exception of Prince Andrew, the Duke of York, of whom she is very fond. Tony Blair himself is invariably cordial and correct in his dealings with Royalty and, according to my informant, he is acutely embarrassed when his wife does little to contribute to the proceedings at Balmoral. He gives the impression that he would be happier in The Queen's company if his wife were not

The Queen used to say that the one place where she could relax completely was onboard the Royal Yacht, Britannia. Sadly the yacht was decommissioned in 1997 and just before that fateful day, the Royal Family set off for their last cruise around the west coast of Britain en route to Scotland. (John Stillwell/PA/EMPICS)

present. On the other hand, she always seems anxious to leave – and some members of the family are equally relieved when she does.

No one has yet revealed whether The Queen and Tony Blair discussed the Ban on Hunting Bill that became law in 2005. If they did it must have been an uncomfortable moment for the Prime Minister as The Queen hunted regularly as a young woman and even after she gave up active participation in the sport, did nothing to discourage her family from hunting.

One of the ways in which The Queen uses her spare time at Balmoral is in signing her 850 Christmas cards. When she had the use of the Royal Yacht *Britannia*, she spent part of the voyage around the west coast of Britain adding her name to the cards before passing them over to Prince Philip for his signature. Now she has to spend the odd afternoon or two doing the same thing at Balmoral.

Moving from Buckingham Palace to Balmoral is a major exercise, with the Army transporting the tons of luggage needed for the Royal Family and the eighty domestic staff who accompany them. The Master of the Household arranges the train journeys and flights, in conjunction with his colleagues, the Crown Equerry and the Captain of the Royal Squadron. The Queen knows that most of her staff enjoy the break almost as much as she does and she goes out of her way to make sure they have as much free time as possible. The staff accommodation at Balmoral has improved immeasurably in recent years, though it still has some way to go before it matches that at Buckingham Palace. But at least now they have heating, whereas in the early days of The Queen's reign, although log fires were burnt throughout the summer months, the place was freezing. The plumbing has also improved so there is no longer a mad rush in the mornings to make sure one has hot water for a bath and shave.

The Balmoral estate is littered with houses and lodges which are used by family and Household for a variety of purposes. Craigowan is a solid stone-built house and is often used by the Royal Family when they make short private visits that do not warrant opening up the castle. Prince Charles and Princess Diana stayed there several times and Princes William and Harry have often invited friends to join them there for a shooting weekend. The Queen's Private Secretary also occupies Craigowan for the entire summer break while he is on duty.

The best-known house on the Balmoral estate is Birkhall, which for many years was the comfortable summer home of the late Queen Elizabeth the Queen Mother. The Queen has a particular affection for Birkhall as she and Prince Philip used it a lot in the first years of their marriage. Then when Elizabeth II acceded to the throne she moved back to the 'big house' and her mother took over the more elegant Birkhall. Once a week The Queen would go over to see her mother for tea and often took guests if she thought Queen Elizabeth (always called that to differentiate from her elder daughter who is simply The Queen) might find them congenial company.

When the Queen Mother died, the house was passed to her favourite grandson, Prince Charles, who gave carte blanche to his companion, Mrs Parker Bowles, to completely refurbish the interior. Hundreds of thousands of pounds have been spent, but Birkhall does not belong to the Prince. It is still the property of The Queen. Ironically, when Queen Victoria

Opposite: Everyone knows of The Queen's love for her corgi dogs and she does not like anyone else to handle them, and she enjoys few things more than walking her dogs in the grounds of one of her homes. (PA/EMPICS)

first bought the house in 1849, it was as a gift for her eldest son, the Prince of Wales, later Edward VII. But again he wasn't given it as an outright present, just allowed to use it as a grace and favour residence.

The Queen calls her annual visit to Balmoral 'hibernating', a time when she can get away from most of the duties that occupy her days during the rest of the year. There are still calls on her, of course. She is Patron of the Highland Cattle Society, a role she takes very seriously and her own Balmoral herd has been highly successful in breeding champions. She also breeds Highland ponies with equal success and she always takes her gun dogs with her on visits to Balmoral. They don't get on too well with her corgis, and neither do the staff. The corgis are a law unto themselves and not all are fully housetrained, so a supply of soda water and blotting paper is always kept on hand to deal with any little 'accidents'.

An even bigger nuisance to the estate is the 4,500 red deer who roam the woods. Fences have been erected to keep them out of areas where they can cause the most damage but every year the factor and his team are kept busy repairing broken gates and fences and patrolling the woods where the deer feed.

At the end of the holiday, the staff hold a fancy dress dance and The Queen and Prince Philip nearly always manage to put in an appearance – but not in fancy dress themselves. The more outrageous and original the outfit, the better The Queen likes it. Nothing and nobody is 'off-limits', but so far no one has had the courage to dress up as 'the boss'. That would really be seen as lese-majesty and Elizabeth II would definitely not be amused.

SIX

The Backroom *Boys*

The names Richard Luce and Robin Janvrin are relatively unknown in Britain, and that's the way both men like it. They prefer their identities to be hidden from public gaze, even though every newspaper editor, reporter and photographer knows exactly who they are and what they do. So, too, do the Prime Minister and the heads of every government department and all senior civil servants.

Richard Luce, a former Conservative Member of Parliament for twenty-one years, is now Lord Luce and, as Lord Chamberlain, is the titular Head of the Royal Household, responsible to The Queen for the six departments that make up her Household. He is the person who reads out the names of those men and women who are receiving honours at the twenty-two Investitures held at Buckingham Palace every year and who had to learn to walk backwards when he got the job. A previous holder of the post passed on the secret of how to stay in a straight line, 'Simply follow the pattern on the carpet.' And while the Lord Chamberlain is the figure at the top of the tree within the Household, he is not the most influential or important. The Queen's Private Secretary and the Keeper of the Privy Purse (unofficially, the holder of the Royal chequebook) are far more important in the league of backroom boys.

Lord Luce has apparently no idea how he became Lord Chamberlain. A one-time Foreign Office minister, he was also Governor of Gibraltar for three years, and was not interviewed by The Queen or anyone in the Royal Household before being appointed. The Prime Minister was not consulted, nor was the Archbishop of Canterbury. There wasn't even a shortlist on which Lord Luce's name appeared. In all probability, his immediate predecessor suggested to The Queen that he would make a good Lord Chamberlain and obviously she agreed. Whatever the route by which he arrived at the Palace, the first time he met The Queen as Lord Chamberlain was on his first day in the post. He was never given a job description or told if it was a full-time post or part-time, nor how many days a week he was expected to work, merely that The Queen had approved his appointment and he was expected to get on with the job. There was nothing unusual in this, it is exactly the way all previous Lord Chamberlains have been appointed and, almost without exception, they have been extremely successful.

The way in which different Lord Chamberlains have approached the post has varied; most have regarded it as an honorary, part-time position and have learned to keep out of the way of the day-to-day running of the Palace. There is a Lord Chamberlain's Office with a large staff, but this is chiefly the responsibility of the Comptroller, who is a full-time employee of The Queen. The only Lord Chamberlain who made it a full-time job was the late Lord (Chips) Maclean, a former Chief Scout, who had no outside business interests, so had nothing to occupy him apart from his Royal duties. He was very surprised to get the job, as he wasn't even a peer at the time. That little problem was soon solved simply by sending him to the House of Lords where he sat on the cross-benches. He became a familiar and popular figure around the Palace, and across the road in St James's Palace where the Royal Collection is housed. He would often pop in to chat to the staff and his friendly approach soon endeared him to everyone he came in contact with.

Previous Lord Chamberlains had been distant figures from old, aristocratic families long associated with Royalty who rarely mixed with members of the Household, not even with senior aides of many years' service. Today, as with all appointments in the Royal Household, the Lord Chamberlain is not expected to come from a small group of the 'right' families with that as the only qualification. The Palace is now run as a meritocracy and accountants and administrators who have business degrees hold senior positions in every department.

Without doubt the most influential figure in the Royal Household is The Queen's Private Secretary, Sir Robin Janvrin. Beginning in the press office, Sir Robin rose to his present position entirely on merit and The Queen has recognised his worth with a number of honours, including making him a Knight Commander of the Royal Victorian Order, her personal Order of Chivalry. (Tim Graham/Getty Images)

Robin Janvrin, now Sir Robin Janvrin, GCVO, CB, is The Queen's Private Secretary and is far and away the most important person in the Palace. He is Her Majesty's closest aide and the man who advises her on all matters. As the conduit between the Monarch and the Prime Minister no premier worth their salt fails to recognise his value.

Nobody, not even the Lord Chamberlain, gets to see The Queen without the Private Secretary knowing about it – there's no question of simply popping his head around her door for a chat. Sir Robin is the keeper of Her Majesty's official diary and accompanies her on all overseas visits. His is the classic case of someone who arrived at the Palace in a modest capacity, was immediately recognised as a 'high-flyer' and rapidly promoted to the position he holds today. He joined the Household as number three in the press office, a comparatively lowly position. Within months he had become The Queen's press secretary before being moved into her private office as one of two assistant private secretaries. He became number two to Robert (now Lord) Fellowes, brother-in-law to the late Diana, Princess of Wales, and when Fellowes left to return to the City, Robin Janvrin was the obvious candidate for the top job.

His term of office has seen some of the most turbulent times in recent Royal history as well as some of the most significant. The incredible wedding fiasco of the Prince of Wales and Mrs Camilla Parker Bowles was a public relations disaster for the Royal Family, including The Queen, through no fault of her own. The differences between her Household and that of Prince Charles across the road in Clarence House became public knowledge through a series of decisions that would never have happened had the arrangements been left in the capable hands of Robin Janvrin and his team. But such was the dislike, even hatred, by Charles's staff for their opposite numbers in Buckingham Palace there was no chance of cooperation between them. The result was that everyone concerned, including The Queen and Prince Philip, were held up to public ridicule.

The significant events of the past few years that have been handled by Robin Janvrin and his staff include the celebrations for The Queen's Golden Jubilee Year in 2002, which were a great success, and two of the saddest occasions when Princess Margaret and the Queen Mother died within weeks of each other.

A successful Private Secretary has to be able to draw the line between sycophancy, which some people believe is the way the Royal Family likes to be treated, and honesty. There have been Private Secretaries in the past who told The Queen only what they thought she wanted to hear, rather than what she ought to hear. Janvrin and his immediate predecessor Robert Fellowes have taken the latter stance. It hasn't always been popular with their Royal mistress but she has recognised the value of their advice and generally accepted it, albeit at times reluctantly.

Within the Private Secretary's Office are a number of smaller sub-departments that answer directly to him. The Queen's press secretary together with her team of assistants, information officers and the staff who look after the Royal website are part of the Private Secretary's Office, so, too, are the Royal Travel Office and the Defence Services Secretary, a senior officer who handles liaison between the Palace and all service units in Britain and the Commonwealth.

The Private Secretary to The Queen also holds the title of Keeper of the Royal Archives, but the day-to-day activities of this department are left in the hands of the Assistant Keeper, based in the Round Tower at Windsor Castle. Scholars, students and authors who request permission to use the archives for serious research purposes are allowed at times to use the facilities, under strict supervision. They are not permitted to remove any document from the building, though photocopying will be done on their behalf, all notes must be taken in pencil, and where the books, papers and photographs they may want are very old, great care has to be taken not to damage the fabric. Working conditions in the Round Tower are pleasant except there are a hundred stone steps to climb from the entrance, so first-timers are advised to take with them all they need.

So far, the Private Secretary has always been a man as The Queen is known to prefer the company of men, even among her staff, but a female assistant private secretary, Mary Francis, was employed on secondment from a government department and was considered a great success until she returned to her old job. If The Queen has an engagement in Britain the Private Secretary does not automatically accompany her. Occasionally one of his staff will be in attendance. As the virtual 'chief executive' of House of Windsor plc he needs to be at his desk throughout the day. But for all major visits including every State Visit overseas, he is always at her side. At the beginning and end of the day he addresses her as 'Your Majesty'. When he sees her at other times of the day it is 'Ma'am'.

A good Private Secretary is invaluable, not only to The Queen but also to the rest of the Household. He is able to gauge her moods and let them know the right time to propose a particular course of action. He is involved in every aspect of Palace life and much of his success depends on his ability to anticipate any problems that might arise and to take appropriate action before they do. He also needs to develop a thick skin and be prepared to stand and listen on occasion to a torrent of verbal abuse from various members of the Royal Family. Every Private Secretary to date has experienced the humiliation of being forced to stand silent without answering back – even when they have been in the right. It is one aspect of life in Royal service that never changes.

Altogether there are six departments in the Royal Household; in other words, The Queen's backroom: the Lord Chamberlain's Office, the Private Secretary, the Keeper of the Privy Purse, the Master of the Household, the Royal Collection and the Crown Equerry.

The Lord Chamberlain's Office handles all ceremonial aspects of Her Majesty's public duties. They organise the Investitures held at Buckingham Palace, with one each at the Palace of Holyroodhouse in Edinburgh and Cardiff Castle in Wales. The Central Chancery of the Orders of Knighthood is the office that has responsibility for the insignia for all the Orders of Chivalry, modest MBEs (Members of the British Empire) to KGs (Knights of the Garter). Eleven staff are employed within this department where they maintain a record of every man and woman who has ever received an honour. And the records are kept indefinitely.

Another of the Lord Chamberlain's duties is to send out the 40,000 or so invitations every summer to the Garden Parties. Every invitation is written in long hand by one of the eight 'temporary lady clerks', some of whom have been 'temporary' for more than twenty years. The clerks are very careful about checking the right spelling and correct title of each would-be guest and the invitation is always sent to the lady of the house. If she is married, her husband may accompany her but the invitation is in her name. This even applies to the Prime Minister. So Mrs Blair would be asked and Tony is included as her escort.

Invitations to Garden Parties are highly sought after but lobbying is a sure way to make sure you do not receive an invitation. The Garden Party Office (it is located in a small building inside St James's Palace) maintains a list of those who have tried to get in through influence or through the back door. There is a 'black list' that now fills five cabinets and people on it are never invited in the future. There have even been occasions when the clerks have been offered bribes to put certain names on the invitation list and – more sinisterly – they regularly receive anonymous letters from people naming others who might be eligible but about whom the writer claims to have evidence of 'unsuitability'. Every one of these letters, as unsavoury as they might be, is investigated and if the accusations are found to be untrue, the invitation stands. The letters themselves are kept indefinitely in one of the locked cabinets in the Garden Party Office and never once has one of the lady clerks succumbed to the temptation of accepting a 'gift' from someone who wants to be included.

Newcomers to the Royal Household are quickly made aware of The Queen's likes and dislikes. She does not care for facial hair, so no one who works closely for her wears a beard; she is not all that keen on moustaches either. Neither does she like men, apart from her footmen, wearing three-piece suits. She feels they are a throwback to an earlier age, so waistcoats (or vests as they are called in the United States) are out. Her Private Secretaries all know she likes to see them with their jackets buttoned. Only her police officers wear them unbuttoned in order to reach their shoulder holsters more easily. She hates the Hilton Hotel in nearby Park Lane, because it towers above the Palace and guests in the upper floors can see into her garden. She enjoys gossip, but only from her dressers, who are her closest female servants. There is a network of informers who keep her fully up to date with all that is happening, not only inside Buckingham Palace, but at all other Royal residences as well. And she can get quite annoyed if she hears from an outsider something that one of her dressers should have told her earlier.

Her senior staff have come to recognise her moods. If she is angry she might say, 'That was an interesting experience.' What she means is 'Under no circumstances, let that happen again.' She also has a disquieting way of showing her disapproval of a suggestion, either from one of her courtiers, or even from a senior politician or prime minister. If she doesn't like the idea she will not say so, she simply doesn't say anything, there is absolute silence. One of her former prime ministers, the late Lord Callaghan, told me it was one of the most intimidating experiences of his political life.

Of the 339 full-time employees at Buckingham Palace, plus an extra 50 or so belonging to the Department of the Environment, who work there permanently looking after the fabric of the building, fewer than a dozen see The Queen on a daily basis. She doesn't hold a morning briefing meeting with her staff and only her Private Secretary, the Master of the Household and her personal servants – dressers, housemaids, footmen and pages – come into contact with her regularly.

All those employed in the Palace know how to behave if they do meet The Queen during the day. They stand still until she has passed and do not speak unless she addresses them first, which she usually does. In the old days, maids and footmen were ordered to hide behind curtains if they saw any member of the Royal Family approaching and any maid who had not finished her morning's work by midday was liable to instant dismissal.

The only time every member of the Household sees The Queen is when she presents them with their Christmas gift during the week before she leaves for Sandringham for the holidays. The routine is strictly adhered to with rigid class segregation enforced at the presentation ceremony. Each member of staff is given the same gift regardless of rank. For Christmas 2005 it was a silver-plated clock marked with the Royal Cypher. Then on the appointed day they all gather in the Bow Room with the members in front, followed by the senior officials and officials, with finally the staff – the cooks, chauffeurs, footmen and housemaids – bringing up the rear. The Master of the Household calls out the name of the recipient, The Queen hands over the gift and says a few words to the lucky man or woman, who thanks her and says it was just what they wanted.

It is not difficult to get a job working for The Queen. One senior footman, who still works at the Palace, told me, 'It's harder to get a job at McDonalds than it is here.' This was proved a couple of years ago when a tabloid newspaper reporter infiltrated the Household and obtained a job as a footman – and later took secret pictures of several of the private apartments.

There is still an enormous prestige in working at Buckingham Palace but even though Her Majesty is regarded as a model employer in many ways, providing uniforms for those who need them, three free meals a day and a subsidised bar where a large gin and tonic costs only £1 and, a recent addition, a 'cybernet' café, plus accommodation at the best address in the world, what she doesn't offer is high wages. A junior footman starts on around £200 a week, out of which he pays 17 per cent rent for his room. And even at the top of the ladder, domestic servants with more than twenty years' service, only earn a little over £20,000 a year. The highest paid members of the staff are the private secretaries with The Queen's Private Secretary earning over £150,000 a year, which doesn't compare with what he could make in a similar post in the commercial world outside.

The Queen takes a keen interest in all her staff and if anything occurs that she should know about, the Master of the Household, who is responsible for all domestic matters, brings it to her attention. Where her personal staff is concerned, she is on much more intimate terms without any hint of familiarity. One of her personal footmen told me that she wanted to know all about his family: his parents, siblings and even his animals, and when he brought his mother and father on a visit to Windsor, The Queen joined them and chatted informally for over half an hour. He said he saw nothing unusual in this as he had been close to The Queen for a few years, but his father was struck dumb at being in the presence of the Sovereign.

On another occasion, he mentioned to Her Majesty that one of the family's dogs had cut his paw and nothing could heal it. She immediately gave him some of her own homeopathic ointment and told him to wrap the injured paw in a soft cloth, such as a torn strip from an old pillowcase, and leave it for a couple of days. He followed her advice and it worked. When he reported back to The Queen she said that she used it when she cut herself and, 'if it works for me, it should work for the dogs'.

The same footman told me that sometimes he felt very sorry for The Queen because she seemed so lonely and there were many occasions when he had served her a light supper on a tray and afterwards she had engaged him in conversation that had lasted for nearly an hour. She was fascinated to hear about his family but never once mentioned her own. It was as if she needed someone to talk to at the end of the day; Prince Philip was out on a private engagement and she was reluctant to be on her own. But he said the following morning it was as if the previous evening had never happened.

Every year a booklet listing all the offices and addresses of members of the Royal Family and their households is circulated throughout the Royal Household. Known as the 'Green Book', simply because that is the colour of the cover, it is a restricted document that many newspaper reporters would pay a fortune to get their hands on as it details, not only the official titles and addresses, but also the names of their spouses and the private telephone numbers. The domestic staff are not listed in the Green Book but two of their members are, without doubt, the most influential of The Queen's personal team, without whom she would find it difficult to function.

Paul Whybrew is The Queen's page, the man closer to Her Majesty than any other male servant in the Royal Household and on whom she relies for her everyday comforts. Mr Whybrew knows all her moods, likes and dislikes, the best time of day to approach her – and, more importantly, when to leave her alone. Technically, he is many rungs of the ladder below the Private Secretaries and press officers, Keeper of the Privy Purse and Crown Equerry, but, in reality, only one other person in the Palace matches his power and influence.

That person is Angela Kelly, The Queen's senior dresser who has now been promoted to the post of personal assistant to The Queen. Angela is an attractive former sergeant in the Women's Royal Army Corps and she has brought her sense of service discipline into the way she runs her department. With two assistants, she looks after all The Queen's wardrobe, but her duties go far beyond being merely the woman who supervises the dressing of her Royal mistress. She is a confidante and companion to The Queen whose loyalty is unchallenged in the Palace. Angela Kelly is a law unto herself and a senior Private Secretary told me: 'We handle her with kid gloves.'

To be The Queen's senior dresser is to see her at her most intimate. No one else, apart from her doctor and, occasionally, her husband, sees The Queen in a state of undress. But it goes much further than that. Angela Kelly has become someone The Queen likes to have at her side; someone she trusts implicitly and who she knows will never betray that trust. Not one of Miss Kelly's friends, either inside or outside the Palace, has ever heard her murmur an indiscreet word about The Queen – and they never will.

She has taken the place of the legendary Bobo Macdonald, who began as a nurse to the infant Princess and remained in Royal service for the rest of her long life, becoming Her Majesty's dresser – and secret informant of all that was going on in every Royal residence. The Queen repaid Bobo's loyalty by installing her in a suite of rooms above her own apartments in Buckingham Palace and providing her with round-the-clock care when she became bedridden in old age. Bobo was an autocratic servant with ideas way above her station – and she got away with it because of her unique relationship with The Queen. Countess Mountbatten once said that when The Queen was coming to stay with her, the problem was not with the guest of honour but making sure Bobo was happy.

Angela Kelly has achieved similar power within the Royal Household. Although her rank places her on the same level as one of the Royal valets, everyone knows that they cross her at their peril. She has the ear of The Queen, more so than the Lord Chamberlain or the Private Secretary, or any of the other titled members of the Royal Household – and both she and they know it.

Another indispensable member of Her Majesty's team is her Page of the Chambers, Ray Wheaton. Now a very senior aide, Mr Wheaton is one of the longest-serving members of the Household, having begun at the bottom as a junior footman, when he could be seen opening the door to visitors at the Privy Purse Entrance. He is now in attendance at all major Royal functions and what he doesn't know about Palace intrigue and the relationship between The Queen and the rest of her staff isn't worth knowing. He is very popular with everyone, from the highest-ranked members of the Royal Household to the various members of the Royal Family, and he is regarded as a future Palace Steward, the pinnacle of achievement for everyone who works on the domestic side of the Palace.

If there is one thing The Queen does not like it is to see strange faces among her Household. She likes familiar people surrounding her at all times. Strangers make her uncomfortable, so the men and women who work most closely with her tend to stay for many years. All of her ladies-in-waiting have been with her for years with some, such as Lady Susan Hussey, being at The Queen's side for more than thirty years. They have become companions. The ladies are much more than mere female assistants, though they do undertake certain tasks on behalf of The Queen, such as answering letters that may have been written by children or the elderly. The Queen does not like these letters to appear too formal, so she prefers one of her ladies-in-waiting to write personally. One occasion when Her Majesty instructed a lady-in-waiting to write a thank-you note on her behalf was after an annual visit to the Chelsea Flower Show. A North Wales seed grower, Medwyn Williams, had sent The Queen some rare blue potatoes she had admired on his stand and offered advice on how they should be cooked. When the lady-in-waiting wrote back she not only thanked Mr Williams for his gift, she also mentioned that The Queen was particularly grateful for the tip about how to cook the potatoes.

The ladies also do any personal shopping The Queen might require, for presents she intends giving to family and friends, as she no longer visits any shops herself although at one time Harrods used to open after hours just for her. They would still be perfectly happy to do so but The Queen does not wish to disrupt normal business hours. There are fourteen ladies-in-waiting headed by the Mistress of the Robes who is always a duchess. She actually has little to do with The Queen's clothes, only supervising the robing of the Sovereign in the Palace of Westminster when Her Majesty formally opens Parliament and attending The Queen on all major overseas tours. The rest of the ladies divide the routine between them and one is always on duty when the Royal Family moves to Sandringham at Christmas, where she joins in all the festivities and eats her meals, including Christmas lunch and dinner, with the family.

In the early days of The Queen's reign, when some of her ladies had young children of their own, Her Majesty insisted that they should not be in attendance during school holidays. It is thoughtfulness like this that provokes the intense loyalty the ladies feel towards The Queen.

Every one of them has been asked personally to become a lady-in-waiting, but the invitation always comes through a third party so that in the event that they do not wish to accept, the refusal is not made directly to The Queen. Embarrassment is thereby spared all round. The ladies are not employees and are not paid a salary but they are reimbursed for any out-of-pocket expenses. They have their own sitting room in Buckingham Palace and eat, when they are on duty, in the Household dining room.

I asked one long-serving lady-in-waiting what were the prime qualifications she and her colleagues needed. She replied, 'A thick skin, as we are treated with a variety of attitudes from utter servility to outright contempt. Some people think we are Royal and curtsy to us; others regard us as skivvies and totally ignore us. Then we have to have a sense of the ridiculous so we can keep a straight face on certain occasions when we are dying to burst out laughing, and finally, a bladder with cast-iron tank-like consistency as we frequently go for what seems like hours without being able to go to the lavatory.' She might have added, the ability to converse with people from all walks of life and from every strata of society. I have watched several ladies-in-waiting when they are with The Queen, and never once have I seen one display any sign of boredom or bad manners, even when I knew they were dying to get back to the Palace for a large gin and tonic.

All the Royal Family, including The Queen, hate the thought of being manipulated into situations where they have to 'perform', which is how they describe some of the duties they are asked to undertake. A favourite response to some of the requests they receive from the media is, 'We do not do stunts.' The Queen is a naturally reticent person who would be perfectly happy if she were never to appear in the media at all. She knows there is no chance of this ever happening. She and her family are news, and what they do is always going to attract public attention.

The Queen is a reluctant celebrity but, as a realist, she knows it is important to accommodate the ladies and gentlemen of the fourth estate from time to time. Which is why there is a press office run at the moment by the first female press secretary The Queen has ever appointed, Penny Russell-Smith. She is efficient, good-humoured and an amiable press officer, a woman who gets on well with the 'Royal' reporters and photographers but who takes no nonsense from any of them, as several have found out when they have tried to get too close to Her Majesty, only to find Miss Russell-Smith physically blocking their path. As one veteran reporter remarked, 'She wields a wicked clipboard.'

One of her tasks is to prepare a digest of press clippings every morning so that The Queen can read them as soon as she starts work. And one of the difficulties she and her predecessors have found is the ambivalent attitude of Her Majesty to press coverage. While she privately feels no compulsion to make headlines, if she has attended a function she regards as important and then the following morning discovers it has not received the attention she feels it deserved, the press secretary feels the icy chill of Royal disapproval.

The Queen and Prince Philip dislike anything that smacks of 'spin-doctoring'. They loathe the idea that anything they do in the way of public duties requires a special glow put upon it. Prince Philip's distrust of the media is well known, and while The Queen accepts there is a need to monitor the press coverage of Royal events, she likes to pretend it has nothing to do with her. In her view the media is a necessary evil; Prince Philip believes fervently it is an entirely unnecessary evil. In spite of this antagonism to the media, there have been press officers at the Palace who have become widely respected and liked by their Royal employers. One such was Ronald Allison, a former BBC reporter who became, arguably, the most successful and well-liked press secretary Buckingham Palace has ever seen. Another, William (now Sir William) Heseltine, progressed from the Press Office to become the most important of The Queen's courtiers, her Private Secretary, as did Sir Robin Janvrin.

Being press secretary at Buckingham Palace is a pretty thankless job. The other senior members of the Royal Household tend to look down slightly on their journalist colleagues, regarding them as 'trade', while the media, with the exception of the Court Correspondent of the Press Association, the only reporter with daily access to the Palace, find they are all treated alike. The Palace shows no favouritism, so nobody gets that exclusive story or picture they all want, in spite of the fact that one or two journalists like to think they are in privileged positions. They are not; all are regarded with equal suspicion and, in many cases, utter contempt.

Most press secretaries leave after five years or so to take up lucrative positions in industry or commerce. They usually receive an honour from The Queen but none has so far been knighted for their service in the press office alone. William Heseltine and Robin Janvrin were both made Knights of the Royal Victorian Order, but not as press secretaries, only when they moved into the Private Secretary's Office. Such are the distinctions made even in The Queen's backroom.

Her Majesty appreciates the hard work carried out by her staff but as she has been at the Palace longer than any of those who work for her, she never places too much reliance on any of them. She knows that the moment one leaves, a replacement will be found. And that applies equally to Private Secretaries as it does to junior footmen and housemaids. There is an apparently unlimited supply of volunteers willing to work for comparatively low salaries but considerable prestige. As one long-serving page told me, 'We used to think we were as easy to replace as a piece of furniture, but we were wrong. The furniture here is regarded as being far more valuable than us. We can easily be replaced; the furniture is priceless and in many cases cannot be replaced.'

* * *

The Queen's working day begins at 9.30 in the morning, after she has been woken by her maid at 7.30 with the 'morning tray' – pots of Earl Grey tea and hot water, fresh milk (from the dairy at Windsor Castle) but no sugar. The cup and saucer are bone china and the crisp linen napkin bears the legend EIIR.

The Roberts radio on her bedside table is permanently tuned to BBC Radio Four, as The Queen likes to be aware of the news from the moment she wakes up. While she bathes in the adjoining bathroom, with its massive cast-iron Victorian bath, the water having been drawn by the maid and tested with a wooden-clad thermometer, one of her three dressers will have laid out the first outfit of the day. Her Majesty never selects the dresses she wears herself; she says that is what she pays her dressers to do – among other things.

Breakfast is at 8.30 and The Queen and Prince Philip usually eat it together – if he is not off on one of his early morning engagements. They do not hang about, and neither do they talk very much, preferring to read the newspapers that have been laid out on a side table, after being ironed to make sure no ink stains Royal fingers.

The Queen's office is a combination of comfortable sitting room and functional study. The colour scheme is green, with several armchairs and sofas upholstered in country-house-style chintz, and the Chinese carpet

Wherever The Queen goes, at home or abroad, in Buckingham Palace, Windsor Castle, Sandringham, Balmoral or even when she was on board the Royal Yacht, her papers follow her everywhere and she spends at least a couple of hours every day working on official documents. For the Sovereign, there is no such thing as a day off. (© Anwar Hussein)

also reflecting the colour in a slightly different shade. It all looks well worn, without in any way being shabby. There is nothing opulent about the room and that is exactly the way The Queen likes it. Her desk is Chippendale and she has had the same one for over sixty years, having brought it from Clarence House when she moved to Buckingham Palace in 1952.

The Queen uses a fountain pen with a thick nib and signs all official documents in black ink. Private correspondence is written in green ink. A fresh sheet of pristine black blotting paper is placed on her desk every morning; black so that no one could read the imprint of her writing even by holding it up to a mirror, and once used it is immediately destroyed by her page. The desk is very cluttered but The Queen knows where everything is and hates things to be moved without her permission. The only concession to twenty-first-century technology is a state-of-the-art telephone system that 'scrambles' her conversation so that no one can eavesdrop when she is talking privately.

The first person she sees every morning once she is ready to begin the day's work is her Private Secretary, Sir Robin Janvrin. His office is immediately below hers on the ground floor and he has been at work since 8 a.m. preparing the day's agenda.

There is a console on The Queen's desk and once she is ready for him she presses a button and says, 'Robin, would you care to come up?' It sounds like a request, but he knows it is the summons he has been waiting for and a few minutes later he knocks discreetly on the door, steps inside, gives a short neck-bow and walks over to join his employer at her desk. He is carrying an ancient wicker basket containing the most important papers requiring Her Majesty's attention. He sits opposite her; her chair is of solid mahogany with an upright back and wide arms. Together they go through the telegrams and official documents that have arrived at the Palace overnight, and which have to be seen by The Queen. He will already have filtered the large amount of mail so that he and his colleagues can handle those that do not need The Queen's personal attention. Through long experience, he knows which ones she wants to read and more importantly those that she has to see. After more than fifty years on the throne, The Queen has developed an amazing ability to scan or speed read documents and the manner in which she is able to master the most complicated briefs has surprised many of her ministers –

particularly those who haven't always done their homework as thoroughly as they should have.

Janvrin explains to The Queen details of the visitors she may be meeting that day and supplements his explanations with short, concise written briefs that Her Majesty will keep near her throughout the day.

If a foreign tour is approaching, Sir Robin will tell Her Majesty how the 'recce' visit went. This is the advance visit by a small party consisting of a member of the Private Secretary's staff, someone from the press office, a lady-in-waiting and one of The Queen's police protection officers. They will carry out the 'recce' several months before the planned visit, going over every minute detail, from the timing of every segment, who is to be presented to The Queen, what the menu is for every meal – with her likes and dislikes noted (no shellfish because of the danger of food poisoning) – the gifts to be exchanged between the Heads of State, whether speeches are expected, if so, how long and in what language (The Queen is prepared to speak in French; the Duke of Edinburgh in French or German).

Hosts are told what the protocol is when being presented to The Queen: she shakes hands with everyone she meets, but no longer demands bows or curtsys and definitely no kissing, even from Gallic hosts for whom this is a normal courtesy. The Director of Royal Travel, a senior member of the Household, confers with the Master of the Household about the requirements of his department for the trip (for a major long-haul overseas tour to somewhere such as Australia and New Zealand, up to forty-five staff will accompany The Queen).

When the final programme is agreed, it is submitted to The Queen for her approval, then copies are sent to the Prime Minister's Office, the Foreign Office and to the embassy or High Commission of the host country. All overseas tours are undertaken on the 'advice' of the Foreign Office and are usually planned at least two years in advance.

Once the programme has been finalised it is printed in a small, pocket-sized booklet called The Blue Book – known unofficially as 'The Bible' – and which is carried by every member of the Household concerned with the tour. Every little detail is listed including the clothes to be worn at each event. These are indicated by a special code: U1 is ceremonial day uniform with decorations and medals; U2 is non-ceremonial day uniform; T1 is tropical day dress, trousers, shirt and tie; T2 is the same but with an open-necked shirt. A capital letter T beside The Queen's name indicates that she will be wearing a tiara.

The Private Secretary and the Master of the Household consult with Her Majesty about the presents she wants to give to her hosts and to those involved in helping to make the arrangements. These are personal mementoes such as signed photographs of herself and Prince Philip in handsome silver or leather frames; the quality depends on the rank of the recipient; gilt cufflinks bearing the Royal cypher and brooches for the ladies. The Queen likes to hand over each gift herself with a word of appreciation towards the end of each tour.

Once the Private Secretary has left to return to his own office, The Queen rings for the duty lady-in-waiting to join her. She is shown a number of letters that Her Majesty feels should be answered in a more personal way than the official replies sent out from the Palace as a matter of course. The lady-in-waiting, who bears the title of Woman of the Bedchamber, writes these letters and signs them on behalf of The Queen. It is a small gesture in itself, but highly appreciated by the recipients and shows how sensitive The Queen is to the feelings of others.

If an Investiture is to take place – and there are some twenty-two each year, which means The Queen has held well over a thousand during her reign – it is held in the State Ballroom at 11 a.m. and lasts for an hour.

Every foreign emissary accredited to the Court of St James's is granted an audience when they arrive in London and when they leave. Each one is given exactly the same amount of time, 10 minutes, and the meetings take place at midday in the Audience Room in the north-west corner of the Palace between the Royal Closet and The Queen's Dining Room, and which is also part of The Queen's suite.

The Queen is Colonel-in-Chief of many regiments and she invariably sees her commanding officers when they assume and relinquish their posts, as well as certain very senior Royal Navy and Royal Air Force officers. The guests are introduced into the Royal presence by the duty equerry, a young officer attached to the Royal Household for three years, one of whose essential attributes must be expertise in social accomplishments, as he needs to be able to get on with people of all ages and from all walks of life. So far The Queen has never appointed a female equerry.

Once a month, The Queen presides over a meeting of the Privy Council in the 1844 Room at Buckingham Palace. The Privy Council is the oldest part of Her Majesty's government, going back to Norman times, and today there are around 400 members as they are appointed for life, so even if the government changes and new members are appointed, the old ones remain privy counsellors. Normally only four or five privy counsellors attend the working meetings which are all conducted with the members and The Queen standing, a practice introduced by Queen Victoria as a mark of respect when her Consort, Prince Albert, died in 1861, and continued ever since. The Queen favours this custom as it has the added advantage of keeping the meetings brief. Among the matters that can be raised – and The Queen is given advance notice by the Clerk of the Council – can be diplomatic immunity, overseas taxation or a list of accomplished legislation. All The Queen has to do is say, 'Approved' after each one, but without her approval these matters do not become law.

The only occasion when the entire Privy Council is summoned is on the Accession of a new Sovereign – as happened in February 1952 – or if an unmarried monarch announces that he or she intends to marry. The only time in the past 200 years that this has happened was in October 1839 when Queen Victoria became betrothed to Prince Albert. When all 400 members are required to be present they hold the meeting in St James's Palace not Buckingham Palace.

After lunch, which is usually eaten alone, and rarely lasts longer than 45 minutes, The Queen likes to walk her corgis in the Palace gardens. She insists on being on her own for the half-hour or so this takes and the only people allowed to remain in the grounds are the gardeners. They have been warned not to acknowledge Her Majesty unless she speaks first but she is never fully alone or out of sight; security men are stationed on the roof of the Palace and they monitor her every move. The Queen says this time in the garden with the dogs is her 'thinking time' when she sorts out some of the problems that have been laid before her and about which she has to decide what action, if any, to take.

Returning to her sitting room, The Queen may relax for a few minutes with the *Sporting Life* or make a few personal telephone calls. It comes as a surprise to many people to hear that Her Majesty is a frequent user of the telephone – but she does not have a mobile and she hates to hear them going off in her presence.

The Queen is joined by Sir Hugh Roberts, Director of the Royal Collection, in the garden at Buckingham Palace as they inspect the grounds in preparation for the summer opening of the State Apartments. (Fiona Hanson/PA/EMPICS)

If there is an afternoon engagement it will always be in the London area and the golden rule is that it must finish before 4.30 so that The Queen can be back in time for tea. It is a ritual that never changes and even though every delicacy imaginable is available, The Queen eats sparingly and most of the goodies, especially the scones, are gobbled up by the corgis. After tea, The Queen works for at least another hour, often until 7 p.m. when she retires to her own rooms to rest before changing for dinner.

On Tuesday evenings, when Parliament is sitting, the Prime Minister is granted an audience of The Queen. It takes place at 6.30, put back an hour from its original timing when Prince Charles and Princess Anne were children because The Queen wanted to spend that time with them, and it has remained at 6.30 ever since. It is a formal occasion, not social, and as such The Queen receives the Prime Minister in the Audience Room, as she does for all other official visitors. No drinks are offered. The purpose is for the Prime Minister to update The Queen on legislative matters and to keep her informed of international affairs involving the United Kingdom. In the last two years, no doubt the problems caused by Britain's continued presence in Iraq and the increased tension in the United Kingdom over terrorist attacks have been high on the agenda.

We shall never know for certain because what happens at the weekly meeting is never revealed. It normally lasts between 30 and 45 minutes and no other person is present. The Queen's Private Secretary entertains his opposite number at No. 10 in his room downstairs and no notes are taken of the meeting between the Prime Minister and the Sovereign. It is entirely confidential though it would be naive not to suppose that the principals do not later keep their Private Secretaries informed of what has transpired.

Every evening a report of the day's proceedings in Parliament is delivered to The Queen. It is written by the Vice-Chamberlain of the Household, a serving Member of Parliament. But nowadays they do not have to write the whole text in longhand as they once did. Instead, a word processor is used and the report is electronically transmitted to Buckingham Palace in seconds. The Queen never avoids reading it before retiring; neither does she neglect her 'boxes', the official despatch cases that are delivered to her wherever she is in the world and which contain papers requiring her initials on every page.

If there is time to relax, The Queen likes to solve giant jigsaws and attempt crossword puzzles without using a thesaurus, which she says is cheating.

She is usually in bed by 11 p.m., but invariably reads for a while, perhaps a novel with a horse racing theme or a report from her racing manager, sometimes until well past midnight. Often hers is the last light in the Palace to be extinguished. And of course she knows that tomorrow she will have to do the whole thing all over again.

The Sport of
seven
Queens

When The Queen and Prince Philip sit down to breakfast, he scans all the daily papers, usually with a smattering of expletives as he spies an item he particularly disagrees with, while The Queen sits quietly reading her favourite paper from cover to cover.

The newspaper in question is the *Racing Post* – the 'bible' of the horse racing fraternity – and no morning can begin without a close inspection of its columns and articles. Her Majesty reads it avidly wherever she is in the world; at home it is delivered to her every day, and if she is abroad, a copy will be sent by wire. If she didn't find it next to her plate, breakfast would be ruined.

A member of the Royal Family and another of the Household have both said that there are only two people in the world who can be put straight through to The Queen at any time. They are her National Hunt adviser, Sir Michael Oswald, who for many years was the late Queen Mother's racing manager until her death in 2002, and who took over the running of the Royal Stud at Sandringham in 1970 until 1999, and John Warren, son-in-law of the late Earl of Carnarvon, who died of a heart attack on the morning of the Twin Towers disaster in New York on 11 September 2001. His death had nothing to do with the disaster; it was just a tragic coincidence. 'Porchy' Carnarvon, as he was known to The Queen – 'Porchy' came from the fact that until he inherited the earldom, he was Lord Porchester – was not only Her Majesty's racing manager, he was one

The Queen has always enjoyed her visits to Kentucky in the United States, the home of thoroughbred racehorses. Here, she is seen with her National Hunt adviser, Sir Michael Oswald, and her hosts, Mr and Mrs William Farish. (Courtesy of Sir Michael Oswald)

of her oldest and truest friends. He was with her on VE Day in 1945 when she and Princess Margaret slipped out of the Palace and mingled with the crowds in The Mall calling for the King. His death was felt deeply by Her Majesty and she still misses him enormously. The reason why she no longer has any one person designated as 'racing manager' is out of respect for Lord Carnarvon's memory. The two men mentioned above are in all respects her racing managers but they are called 'advisers'.

The Queen's love of horses has been well documented. Her father had instilled it in her since childhood when she was first taken to the Royal stables at Beckhampton in Wiltshire. A story that has gone the rounds in Royal circles for over sixty years has it that the young Princess Elizabeth once stroked a classic winner at the stables and was so impressed that she didn't wash her hand for a week.

Although she was first put into the saddle almost before she could walk, she was taught to ride properly in 1938 by Horace Smith, to whom she confided that 'had she not been who she was, she would like to be a lady living in the country with lots of horses and dogs'. It was Smith who also taught the young Princess to ride side-saddle, a skill she later needed as Queen, when she rode her horse Burmese to the annual Trooping the Colour Parade on Horseguards. And never more so than on 13 June 1981 when a gunman fired blank cartridges at her as she was about to turn into Horseguards from The Mall. Everyone remembers her coolness on that day when she controlled Burmese brilliantly and continued with the parade as if nothing had happened.

Racing has been a passion of The Queen's throughout her adult life. She was given her first racehorse, Astrakan, as a wedding present in 1947 by the Aga Khan, and since then she has owned and bred scores of thoroughbreds. Her ambition, and that of everyone connected with her racing interests, is to win the premier flat race, the Derby. So far she has been unsuccessful with her best chance to date being in 1953 when the race was run the day following the Coronation. Her horse Aureole was strongly fancied but came second to Pinza. In 1954, Aureole won the King George VI and Queen Elizabeth Stakes at Ascot, but it was small consolation after the Derby disappointment.

Royal Ascot is an important part of the Royal calendar with a large house party being held throughout the week at Windsor Castle. Every afternoon before racing starts, The Queen, Prince Philip and their guests drive in an open carriage procession down the course before going into the Royal Box to watch the races. Henry Kissinger and his wife were guests on one occasion and he said it was one of the highlights of his life. 'I never thought for one moment that I would ever be sitting in a carriage with The Queen and Prince Philip, being driven by a liveried coachman in front of the grandstands at Ascot.'

The organisation of The Queen's house party during Ascot Week involves the Master of the Household, the Crown Equerry, Her Majesty's personal equerry, The Queen's representative at Ascot and other members of the Household. The Royal Box (demolished in 2005 to make way for a newer, grander building) is located right on the finishing line. Luncheon is always taken at Windsor Castle before the afternoon drive down the course. The guests join Her Majesty in the Royal Box where there are two banks of seats. The Queen always sits in the front row in the seat on the extreme

Whenever The Queen has the opportunity, she likes to visit her racing stables to check on the form and progress of her horses. Her trainers and jockeys say she is one of the most knowledgeable owners in the world and she doesn't stand on ceremony when she is with them. (Courtesy of Sir Michael Oswald)

right-hand side. This gives her the best view of the finishing straight. When they retire for tea, it is served in a dining room on the same floor as the viewing area, where liveried footmen have laid eight round tables.

The Queen sits with up to seven guests, all of whom have been personally chosen by her. Members of the Royal Family host the other tables and the Master of the Household tells the guests where they should sit. No one has to look for a place; he has allocated them all. Apart from those guests who are in the Royal party, Her Majesty also invites several others to join her for tea. There is a certain amount of formality, but the atmosphere is very relaxed and The Queen encourages conversation, so no one has to wait to be spoken to before speaking themselves. The meal is superb: exquisite sandwiches, all with the crusts cut off, several different kinds of cake and gateaux, and strawberries and cream. All served on the finest bone china and eaten with solid silver cutlery.

Throughout Ascot Week, the diminutive figure of The Queen dominates the social scene. She is the living embodiment of the sport of kings – and queens – and it is one of the few times when spectators might see her rushing from the rear of the Royal Box to the front to see the winner crossing the finishing line. She is said to have a quicker eye than the official photo-finish equipment and her guests are amazed at how often she comes up with the right horse even before it has been announced.

Many of her oldest friends are equally enthusiastic about racing and she greets them warmly as she processes regally to the paddock, gracefully acknowledging the courtly bows and curtsys from members of the aristocracy and fellow racegoers alike. It's a bit like an exclusive 'old boys' club, with, on this occasion, the senior member being an 'old girl'. Many people have wondered if The Queen is tempted to 'have a flutter' when one of her fancied horses is running. The answer is no, she never bets, but she does buy a ticket for the sweepstake that is run in the Royal Box (but only on Derby Day, not Royal Ascot) and she has held the winning ticket a number of times. However, the prize money rarely rises above £25 as the tickets cost only £1 each.

One of The Queen's favourite pastimes during Ascot Week was to canter down the course in the early morning, accompanied by some of her house guests, before the crowds arrived. But the media got to hear of it and made it impossible for Her Majesty to enjoy her ride. She steadfastly refused to wear a protective hard hat, as the jockeys have to, preferring a silk headscarf. This inevitably attracted criticism from a certain section of the public, and the media, as does the fact that she won't wear a seat belt when driving herself on the private roads of her estates.

The Queen is very much a 'hands-on' owner and breeder of racehorses. She is not content to sit back and let her advisers tell her what to buy and when to run her horses. She reads the formbooks and knows exactly what she wants. She also has a photographic memory so she is able to recall events from years past and how one of her horses performed on those occasions. And in precisely the same way that all her prime ministers have found when they have not done their homework completely, she will soon correct her racing team if she thinks they are wrong and remind them that such and such a horse 'didn't run all that well at York in 1995. Don't you remember?'

As previously mentioned, Sir Michael Oswald was the Queen Mother's racing manager for many years, having started in the business as a stud pupil and worked his way to the top. Both the Oswalds have impeccable credentials to be Royal aides, as Sir Michael's wife, Lady Angela, a daughter of the 6th Marquess of Exeter, was a Woman of the Bedchamber to Queen Elizabeth the Queen Mother.

Queen Elizabeth was a great patron of steeplechasing and hurdling, and Clarence House was the only private home in London to be equipped with a 'blower' communication system that carried the results directly from the racecourse.

When Her Majesty died, representations were made to The Queen that it would be nice if the Royal Family could retain a presence in steeplechasing. She agreed and now has a small team of hurdlers and steeplechasers, all of whom are trained by Nicky Henderson at Lambourn. On the flat, The Queen has around thirty horses in training, which, as Michael Oswald explains, places her nowhere near the top of the major players in the game.

Her Majesty and Sir Michael Oswald discussing the progress of one of her racehorses. They talk most days, particularly when she has a horse running, and he is one of the few people who can always be put through to her. (Courtesy of Sir Michael Oswald)

When The Queen came to the throne, there were thirty or so important owner/breeders in Western Europe: Britain, Ireland, France, Italy and Germany. Today very few are left. Probably no more than five or six, with the Aga Khan, Prince Khalid Abdullah of Saudi Arabia and the four Maktoum brothers being highly successful, each with around 200 brood mares and a further 250 in training. And there is a huge operation in Ireland where the Coolmore Stud is said to be the largest in the world. Which makes them at least ten times bigger than The Queen and in terms of money invested, thirty or forty times larger.

Obviously The Queen cannot match these people in numbers, with all the money that's expended. The Royal studs have always been run as commercial enterprises and they have always paid their way, so it's absolutely right that Her Majesty keeps the whole operation down to its present level and aims for quality not quantity. It's all very well for people to ask, 'Why doesn't The Queen win the Derby?' They seem to forget that in racing terms she is a comparatively small fish in what is now a very large international pond.

On the other hand, The Queen is a very astute owner and investor. At the Royal stud there is one stallion standing named Royal Applause. He is the stud's biggest single earner and The Queen personally owns part of him. The rest belongs to the Maktoum family. The fee for Royal Applause is around £20,000 and in a season he will cover some 130 mares, so there are total earnings of £800,000 from that one stallion alone.

One thing that everyone connected with The Queen's racing has to be very sure of is that not one penny comes from the public purse. It is an entirely private enterprise and as far back as 1976 the Royal stud at Hampton Court was closed to thoroughbreds to avoid any possibility of charges being laid that public money was being used to prop up The Queen's racing activities. If one of the walls surrounding the Hampton Court stud needed repairing or one of the gates had to be painted, the Ministry of Works carried out the job – and paid for it out of public funds. So The Queen's racehorses had to be moved. The Royal Mews horses could safely be stabled there as they are State horses, but not those owned privately by The Queen or her family. The financial strictures are so severe that even the postage stamps on envelopes used for stud business are paid for separately, unlike all other official mail, which is stamped with the Royal cypher.

The Queen has been sending mares to the United States for many years. Just after the Second World War most of the best stallions in the world found their way to America and by the time The Queen came to the throne, she knew she should be thinking of sending a mare or two across the Atlantic. The first to be sent was in the early 1960s and then in the 1970s some more went – at first it was two at a time, then three, and finally in the 1980s half a dozen mares went to Alice Chandler at Mill Ridge near Lexington, a principal area for thoroughbred breeding, not only in the United States but the whole world, and to Will Farish at Lanes End which is also near Lexington. Will Farish, a former US Ambassador to the Court of St James's, is an old friend of The Queen and she has stayed at his home several times.

A delighted younger Queen following a successful day's racing. There are few things guaranteed to please her more than when one of her horses is first past the winning post. (Courtesy of Sir Michael Oswald)

Michael Oswald explained that when a mare is sent to America, it stays for perhaps three or four years. She is covered by a stallion and any foals she has as a result are brought back to Britain once they have been weaned to be installed in the Royal stud.

There is no doubt about The Queen's knowledge of her sport. 'She is incredibly knowledgeable,' Sir Michael says, 'and one has to be very thorough before, for example, going to one of the Newmarket December sales because she is likely to ask about a particular lot and when you wonder why she should be curious about that one, you suddenly find way back in the catalogue that she has had something to do with the pedigree. She has a tremendous knowledge of pedigrees and not only of her own horses.'

But what is the attraction for her in what is a very competitive sport? Those who work closely with her believe it is an extremely therapeutic exercise. There are always papers waiting for her. Even when she is on holiday at Balmoral or Sandringham, she is never very far away from a Private Secretary who is likely to pop up with a box full of papers to be looked at and signed. The work never goes away. So racing, which she knows so much about, like her gun dogs, is a subject she can be totally immersed in and which is completely different. She loves to go around a stud or racing stable and watch horses working and she can take part in a discussion on what can mate with what. For 2 or 3 hours she can almost, but not quite, forget the cares of monarchy. It is a very valuable therapy and one of her Private Secretaries says he thinks it is exactly that.

So how much time does Her Majesty spend on racecourses? Not all that much. In fact, there are only seven days in the year that are ring-fenced in her diary for racing. First is the Derby, then the five days of Royal Ascot (in 2005 it was transferred to York because of the rebuilding at Ascot) and the Saturday of the King George VI and Queen Elizabeth Stakes. Those are the only immovable dates in the Royal calendar. Any extra days are all really a matter of luck and have to fit in with where she is and what her duties are likely to be. If she happens to be at Windsor and has a horse running there, or somewhere close and accessible such as Newbury, Sandown or Kempton, she might go, but it doesn't happen very often.

Her advisers are expected to offer their very best opinions to The Queen, but is Her Majesty good at taking advice? A question I put to Sir Michael Oswald: 'The answer is she is, but she will certainly tell you in no uncertain terms if she disagrees with what you say. You have to make a good case and she will always allow you to present it. You get a fair hearing. But if she thinks you are talking absolute rubbish, then she'll tell you very firmly and, of course, the ultimate decision is always hers; it has to be.'

The Queen likes to name all her horses herself. The Princess Royal once said her mother was rather innocent in some ways and she occasionally has to have it pointed out to her that a name she has selected might not be suitable if a double entendre can be found. The Queen Mother used to say to her, 'Oh. You can't have that one. Imagine how it will sound when the commentator says it out loud.'

Among The Queen's trainers have been some of the truly illustrious names in racing. In the early days of her reign, Captain Sir Cecil Boyd-Rochfort and Sir Noel Murless trained for her at Newmarket. Then came Peter Hastings Bass and his son-in-law, Ian Balding, at Kingsclere, followed by Major Dick Hern whose stables were at West Ilsley. William Hastings Bass, now the Earl of Hartington, was another successful trainer for Her Majesty and at present there are four men involved in The Queen's flat training programme: Sir Michael Stout at Newmarket; Roger Charlton at Beckhampton; Richard Hannon, who trains at Marlborough and Andrew Balding, brother of Clare Balding, who presents the BBC's racing coverage, at Kingsclere.

Although The Queen has had a racing manager, trainers and now both National Hunt and flat racing advisers, she has never employed any single Royal jockey as such. All the greats have ridden for her: Lester Piggott, Sir Gordon Richards, Joe Mercer, who gave The Queen one of her early classic winners when he rode Highclere to victory in the One Thousand Guineas in 1974, when she also won the French classic *Prix de Diane*. So it was a profitable year for Her Majesty as her horses won over £140,000 that season. Willie Carson, Harry Carr and Doug Smith have also all ridden for her but none has been described as THE Royal jockey. The reason is that the first or senior jockey at whichever stable The Queen is using, usually rides for Her Majesty.

In fact, there is only one person who can be accurately called the Royal jockey and that is The Queen's daughter, the Princess Royal. She has ridden in The Queen's colours several times and was a very capable – and ultra-competitive – amateur.

Like most owners, The Queen has had mixed fortunes on the turf. As decades go, the 1950s were extremely good, the 1960s less so. The 1970s were highly successful with four classic wins, the 1980s and 1990s pretty fair. As previously mentioned, 1974 was a good year, as was 1977, when she won both The Oaks and the St Leger, and as far back as 1957, she was the leading owner in the country. But there have also been lean spells when she has gone through several seasons without a major winner. Of course in recent years the sport has seen a vastly increased infusion of overseas capital, which in turn has led to greater international competition. The Queen takes it all in her stride. For her, although winning is a bonus of course, she is a true believer in the Olympic ideal that it is the taking part that is important, in spite of the fact that she has a totally professional attitude to her favourite sport.

Prince Philip does not share The Queen's enthusiasm for racing and often if there is a Test match being played during Ascot Week, he will sit at the back of the Royal Box watching on television. He does, however, share The Queen's love of horses. In his case polo was his first love as a younger man, and even now at 84, he still competes energetically in carriage driving. The Queen always supports him

Her Majesty takes a keen interest when any of her family is competing and here she is using her personal camera to record for posterity Prince Philip taking part in a carriage-driving event at the Royal Windsor Horse Show. [Jayne Fincher/© Photographers International]

when he is taking part at Windsor or Sandringham and once when he actually won the event at Sandringham, someone congratulated him and casually mentioned that it was not bad for an old-age pensioner. Although he was 67 at the time, he did not appreciate the comment. What is not generally known is that The Queen was a proficient carriage driver long before her husband. In fact, she won first prize at the Royal Windsor Horse Show two years running: 1943 and 1944. However, she is tactful enough not to mention this in his presence.

The Princess Royal is the only one of Her Majesty's family really to share her devotion to horse racing. The others put in occasional appearances at Ascot and other meetings, but they do not relish a day at the races as she does. And this is one of her concerns, that when she goes, no one else in the family will carry on the Royal tradition of supporting horse racing in Britain. The Prince of Wales loves polo, as do his sons, William and Harry, but none of them has as yet shown any interest in owning and breeding racehorses, either on the flat or 'over the sticks'.

The Queen was welcomed by Professor Sidney Ricketts and Dr Peter Rossdale when she opened the Beaufort Cottage Equine Hospital in April 1998. (Courtesy of Sir Michael Oswald)

In all probability there will always be some sort of Royal presence at Royal Ascot and the Derby, but many people involved in the sport feel it will be a sad day indeed when the *Racing Post* ceases to be required daily reading at Buckingham Palace.

Many of the interests The Queen enjoys – horses, dogs, even the Royal stamp collection – have been inherited from her father, George VI. One such is the Royal Pigeon Loft at Sandringham. It comes as something of a surprise to many people, who imagine that Her Majesty is interested only in sporting pastimes normally associated with the upper classes, that she is an enthusiastic pigeon fancier. This highly specialised sport, whose public image has in the past been traditionally associated with flat-capped working men from the North of England or the South Wales valleys, now attracts people from every class and all walks of life.

The Queen's pigeons, housed in excellent facilities in the home of an established pigeon expert near the Sandringham estate, have been tremendously successful both in Britain and abroad and she is delighted to hear when one of her birds wins yet another competition. The Royal Lofts manager keeps in touch with The Queen through her land agent at Sandringham and if improvements need to be made to the pigeons' accommodation at any time, her approval for the finance is sought.

Her Majesty is not just another wealthy owner who leaves everything to others; she takes a personal interest in the welfare and progress of her pigeons and is kept informed whenever they are racing. She visits the Lofts when she is at Sandringham, but not in the breeding season as she knows this would be an intrusion, and takes great pride in occasionally inviting favoured guests to join her. She also tries to visit the annual Fur and Feather Show in Norfolk when she is able. There is a sense of close if competitive camaraderie among pigeon fanciers and The Queen's patronage of the sport has not only raised its profile but meant other fanciers like to think of her, respectfully, as 'one of us'.

The Royal pigeons all carry the cypher EIIR in the number on their rings and as possession of one of these birds is highly sought after, several go missing every year during their long journeys home. Of course, not all are stolen; many pigeons are lost through straying onto high-voltage electricity cables and others simply join the flocks of pigeons seen scavenging for food on city streets. Every pigeon's official number is logged on a computer and if anyone finds a stray that perhaps is unable to continue its journey they can contact the Royal Pigeon Racing Association so the owner can be informed.

The first Royal birds were the gift of King Leopold of the Belgians to the Prince of Wales (later King Edward VII) in 1886. The Prince had admired Leopold's pigeons on a visit to Belgium and His Majesty immediately despatched some of his birds to Sandringham. There have been Royal Pigeon Lofts in Norfolk ever since, with The Queen's grandfather, King George V, being a particular enthusiast since he began racing pigeons in 1893 when he was Duke of York.

Royal birds have won many prestigious prizes, with the first being in 1899 when the Prince of Wales won the national race from Lerwick in the Shetland Isles – a distance of 515 miles. The Queen handles the birds herself when she visits the Royal Lofts, but unlike her horses, pigeons, even Royal ones, are not named. They are just given a number, but she and the manager of the Royal Pigeon Lofts know every bird individually and can tell immediately if one is missing.

Everyone knows about The Queen's love for her corgi dogs. What few people realise though is that she is also a passionate breeder and trainer of gun dogs. And this pastime is one she practises as a hands-on owner, not just because she has inherited the sport. She breeds both labradors and spaniels at Sandringham and her dogs are worth hundreds of pounds. Her Majesty first showed an interest in training gun dogs when she was a young woman and wanted to be allowed to work the animals herself in the field. However, her father would not permit her to be seen working the dogs alongside everyone else; he thought it an unseemly sport for a future queen to be directly involved in.

When she acceded to the throne, Elizabeth II took control of her own life and almost immediately began to work her dogs at Sandringham and during the long summer break at Balmoral. She quickly became an expert in directing dogs to 'pick up' birds at a shoot and she has an uncanny ability to work a dog that she may not have trained herself; after all, she has a staff to do this at Sandringham throughout the year when she is not in residence.

The standard of the Sandringham gun dogs now ranks among the highest in the world and several have won senior prizes at Game Fairs throughout Britain and achieved champion status at field trials. All of which is very satisfying to The Queen who loves competition and likes to win as much as the next person.

eight

Royal *Style*

None of The Queen's male couturiers – Norman Hartnell, Hardy Amies, Ian Thomas or any of the others – was ever allowed to pass a tape measure around the Royal bust or to see their most distinguished client in a state of undress. It is an unwritten, but nevertheless inflexible, rule that only women are permitted to take The Queen's measurements and to be present in the dressing room when Her Majesty is clad in her undergarments. The men all wait outside until they are called and if alterations are required, they say where but the chalk marks or pins are placed on the Royal torso by a female assistant.

The Queen also will not allow any deprecating remarks to be made in her presence about her choice of clothes. If a designer thinks the material Her Majesty has selected for a particular outfit is not suitable for the occasion, he or she might venture to remark that 'This linen dress might crease Ma'am. Would you prefer to see it in cotton or silk?' And if perhaps The Queen has asked for say extra pockets or a collar that seem to be unnecessary to the designer, it takes great delicacy to suggest that they should be removed. Her Majesty has become so used to having people obey her every wish that she does not welcome criticism from those she employs. She does not rant and rave; that's not her style. But she does have an icy glare that is said to freeze at twenty paces if she thinks someone has overstepped the mark. Not that it happens very often. The

During The Queen's visit to Canada in April 2005, she wore many different outfits, depending on the weather and the location. Here, she is leaving the Legislature Building in Edmonton wearing a pink hat and coat with black accessories. (Fiona Hanson/PA/EMPICS)

Queen has a quiet, courteous manner and manages to make every order sound like a request. But those around her know that they disobey at their peril and once the Royal curtain of disapproval descends it is with chilling finality. The Queen knows instinctively exactly the image she wants to project, both at home and abroad, and she has been steadfast in her choice of wardrobe for sixty years. She deliberately remains apart from current fashion and outside her preferred designers she has stayed loyal to household names such as Burberry and Acquascutum.

When the late Diana, Princess of Wales emerged onto the Royal scene in 1981, she became a fashion icon. Women all over the world followed her style slavishly. She once wore a tiny hat in the style of Robin Hood. Within weeks more than a million copies were sold in Japan alone. She did more to revive British fashion – and particularly millinery – than anyone before or since. She was the first member of the Royal Family to be described as a 'walking clothes horse' though she detested the appellation.

No one would ever call The Queen by that name. Or any other lady in the Royal Family, with the possible exception of her granddaughter Zara Phillips, and she attracts attention more because of her outlandish outfits than her sense of style.

The Queen has always regarded her clothes as part of the job. She has never followed fashion and, indeed, in the early days of her reign her dresses and coats were strictly functional and comfortable. Now in her ninth decade she has at last started to be seen as a woman who can be stylish, even if in the main her image remains as 'sensible and conformist'.

Her Majesty is at heart a countrywoman, more comfortable in headscarves, tweeds and wellington boots than the formal outfits she is required to wear when she is on duty. But it is not true that she is completely uninterested in clothes or that she does not notice what other women are wearing. The Queen takes note of every detail and she knows what suits her. Throughout the fifty-odd years she has been on the throne, the length of her dresses and coats has rarely changed more than an inch. She likes her dresses and skirts to be about halfway between the knee and ankle and there they have remained since 1952.

The Queen's hats have always been a source of comment. She is rarely seen in public without her head being covered; the difficulty for her milliners is that her hairstyle hasn't altered in years and usually it looks as if it has been set in concrete, so they have to compromise when they design hats for her. Also, the hats have to be worn off the face so the public – and photographers – can see her clearly. The late Queen Elizabeth, the Queen Mother, gave her daughter this piece of invaluable advice. No one ever saw the Queen Mother wearing a hat that shielded her face. Of course, her style was unique to her. On anyone else it would have looked ridiculous, those acres of chiffon in those vivid colours, but on her they were perfect. She knew better than any professional designer exactly what suited her – and that's what she wore throughout her long life.

None of the women in the present Royal Family is considered to be stylish. They follow The Queen in that they regard clothes a necessary but troublesome aspect of being Royal. Their clothes are chosen to fulfil certain criteria: they must be suitable for the job, they must also be functional and finally they need to be comfortable. The Princess Royal once told me that 'a good suit can go on for years'. As she was wearing one that was then over twenty years old, I took her point. She added that she always had longer hems than usual on her dresses and skirts so that they could be raised and lowered according to fashion.

The Queen does not insist on having her hems lengthened in the same way, but she does possess outfits that have stood the test of time over many years. I was once visiting Buckingham Palace to see a member of the Royal Household when The Queen passed by in one of the corridors. When I went into the office of the person I was due to see, I mentioned that I thought the dress Her Majesty was wearing was familiar. The courtier, and it was a woman, said, 'It ought to be, it's probably fifteen or sixteen years old. When The Queen is staying in the Palace all day and not seeing anyone particularly important, she will often wear something she has had for years. It's comfortable and that's what counts when she's not on show.'

For the first twenty years of The Queen's reign, she barely changed her style at all. Her sole designer was Norman Hartnell, who had dressed her mother since before the Second World War, and he saw no reason why The Queen should change her style – and evidently she agreed. It was Hartnell who made Princess Elizabeth's wedding dress in 1947 – after he had submitted three different designs from which she made her choice, the final one embroidered with 10,000 American seed pearls. And when she attended the wedding of her sister, Princess Margaret, in 1960, The Queen and the other ladies in the Royal Family all wore full-length gowns – the last time this occurred. They saw nothing strange or outmoded in this, but shortly afterwards Princess Margaret influenced her older sister to engage other designers who brought more modern approaches to the Royal clothes.

The Queen's dressing room overlooks Constitution Hill and Green Park. A large airy room, it has mirrors on every wall so that she and her designers can see the clothes she is wearing from every angle. Her Majesty also has had a dressing table installed in the room fitted with a triple mirror so that she can see for herself how she looks in a particular outfit when she is sitting down. This can be an important point and one of her designers told me it was the idea of The Queen herself. He did not suggest it, but he has since put similar dressing tables in his own salons so that his other clients (they are never called customers) can view themselves from all angles, standing up and sitting down.

The Queen has definite opinions on the colours she wears and often she will ask her couturiers to make something from a bolt of cloth she has been given as a present on one of her overseas visits. If she thinks the colour or pattern is a little too bold for her, she might offer the cloth to her daughter, the Princess Royal, particularly if it is blue or green, the Princess's favourite colours. The Queen prefers pastel shades for herself in the daytime and for more formal wear in the evening it might be emerald or lavender. Her collection of evening gowns is fabulous by any standards, with the dresses running into hundreds. Lately

One of The Queen's favourite dress designers, Maureen Rose, working on a garment for her Royal client.
Mrs Rose worked for Her Majesty for more than twenty years. (Maureen Rose)

Another of Maureen Rose's creations, showing the intricate pattern of embroidery. She says some of the dresses took up to 600 hours of manpower to make. (Maureen Rose)

Every one of the 10,000 beads and pearls on this evening gown were sewn on by hand. It was a proud boast of Maureen Rose that nothing she made for The Queen was ever touched by machine. (Maureen Rose)

she has been persuaded to allow more and more glitter to be added and at evening receptions at Buckingham Palace, she is a vision of shimmering light from tiara-clad head to toe and wearing diamonds from the most stunning private collection in the world.

Maureen Rose, one of Her Majesty's favourite dress designers, began her professional career working for Norman Hartnell alongside Ian Thomas. When Thomas left to start up on his own, he persuaded Maureen to go with him and that was when she made the first of many visits to Buckingham Palace. She recalls that first occasion when she had to fit The Queen:

> It was a very special occasion as I was making a casual evening outfit for Her Majesty and I knew she was anxious for it to be right as the material had been a gift from the King of Thailand. The material wasn't easy to use as it had a border print and you cannot make a dress longer than the print itself. I was very nervous and fussing a bit more than usual, and I had been told before we got there that I would be in the dressing room with The Queen while Ian Thomas waited outside. We had worked out a system whereby he watched the door handle and as soon as I – and The Queen – was ready, I would turn the handle. Once he saw this he could come in. The first thing he said, and remember this was my first Royal visit, was 'That skirt's a little bit too short.' I wanted the floor to open up and swallow me. But The Queen came to my rescue saying 'It would fit perfectly if I had flat shoes on, wouldn't it?' And she smiled at me and the next time I went to fit her she was wearing flat shoes.

It was an example of the perfect manners The Queen displays to men and women who are new to her. The only time she can be short is when she feels she knows you well enough. It is some sort of backhanded compliment. This is common to all the Royal Family. They behave impeccably towards strangers and only let off steam in the company of those with whom they feel comfortable. Princess Anne once had a police bodyguard who was rapidly losing his hair and on one occasion he had done something that irritated her. She said in a tone of resignation, 'It's enough to make you tear your hair out.' Then, looking up at his receding hairline, added, 'Well, it would if you had any.' He didn't feel insulted because he knew she would only have made the remark to him if he were part of her inner circle.

Wherever The Queen goes in the Palace, her corgis go with her. They are inseparable and are rarely out of her sight unless she has a formal duty such as an Investiture in the State Ballroom or a meeting of the Privy Council. The dogs are always around when she is being fitted with new clothes and the dress designers have to be very careful not to upset them as they are a law unto themselves. In the Royal dressing room, assistants make sure every pin or sharp object is picked up from the floor so nothing gets stuck in a tiny paw. The Queen even carries a special magnet around with her and she goes over the carpet with it picking up any stray piece of metal that might injure the corgis. The designers have learned to step carefully around and over the dogs who lie all over the place, and several ankles have been nipped when an unwary leg has come within biting distance. They never complain, because they know the corgis, like The Queen's children, are never in the wrong.

When the late Diana, Princess of Wales first joined the Royal Family, she was photographed coming down the steps of a Royal helicopter when the wind blew her dress up around her thighs. No one has ever had a glimpse of The Queen's upper legs on similar occasions and there has long been a debate about how she manages to keep her skirts down around her knees in even the strongest breeze. Maureen Rose has the answer. And it does not involve sewing lead weights into the hem of the dresses and skirts. 'As many of the dresses are ultra-lightweight anyway, it simply wouldn't work. So I always put in a straight lining, fitted to the body so that even if the dress blew up, the lining wouldn't.'

If there is one thing guaranteed to irritate The Queen it is someone fussing around her. She likes people to be relaxed – or as relaxed as anyone can be in the presence of the Sovereign. This was why she was so fond of the late Sir Hardy Amies, who enjoyed her patronage from 1948 until the day he died in 2003 at the age of 93.

Amies, who was made a Knight Commander of the Royal Victorian Order in 1989 for his services to Her Majesty, was completely different from his immediate predecessor, Norman Hartnell, who was a couturier of the old school in that he treated his clients, all of whom were aristocrats, or very wealthy ladies from old families, with the utmost respect, bordering on servility. He had dressed the Queen Mother for many years and when her daughter ascended the throne, unkind members of the Royal Household said he conducted all his dealings with her 'from a kneeling position'. Hartnell had

The Queen dressed for a formal evening engagement complete with diamond tiara and matching sapphire necklace and bracelet. The chain of her handbag is solid gold. (Jayne Fincher/© Photographers International)

designed the dress The Queen wore for her Coronation in 1953. His designs had barely changed in two decades; the Queen Mother thought he was brilliant and The Queen never thought to question him about the kind of dresses he was making for her. The Royal Household, including those who had spoken of him so disparagingly, hated change anyway; as far as they were concerned he could have gone on designing the same dresses for years.

Hardy Amies was totally different. Tall, elegant and always immaculately turned out himself, he was also a witty and easy conversationalist. The Queen warmed to him from the first moment they met and even though he was clever enough never to confuse her friendliness with familiarity, they established a mutual regard that lasted for fifty years. He was never on edge in her presence, and in the 1950s and 1960s his glamorous designs caused the word 'chic' to be used for the first time by fashion writers in describing Her Majesty's clothes. But Amies concentrated on making classical suits and coats for The Queen, while he left the dresses to other designers.

It is a special honour to be asked by The Queen to design an outfit for a special occasion, such as a State Visit. Maureen Rose made two black dresses for The Queen when she visited Pope John Paul II at the Vatican. The first was in 1980, when Mrs Rose was working with Ian Thomas (who died in 1993), and then again twenty years later when she was working for herself. The State Visit to Italy in 2000 was a triumph for The Queen – and for her designer after the Italian fashion media were ecstatic over some of the clothes Her Majesty wore. Maureen Rose made a heavy ice-blue crêpe evening gown trimmed with silver lace and embroidered with aquamarine which The Queen wore to a State Banquet. The next morning Her Majesty was described in the press as 'The Queen of Fashion', the first and, so far, only time such superlatives have been used in reference to her clothes.

Although The Queen has favourite designers to make certain clothes, she has not since the days of Norman Hartnell employed any of them exclusively. They all know they are not the only men and women making dresses for her, but such is Her Majesty's sense of decorum that whenever a particular designer is summoned to the Palace, she will always be wearing one of their creations and the doors to the wardrobes where clothes by other designers are stored are kept firmly closed. And The Queen never comments about one designer's clothes to another. The fitting sessions can last up to 3 hours at a time and involve six or seven changes of dress for The Queen. She never complains and never asks to sit down. Occasionally, the Duke of Edinburgh might pass through the dressing room. He always acknowledges the people working there but again, never makes the slightest comment about the clothes they are working on. Fitting sessions are extremely tiring for both The Queen and those fitting her. At the end of a long afternoon, while the designers can go home and rest, The Queen often has another function to attend.

Not all fitting sessions take place at Buckingham Palace; occasionally the designers have to wait on Her Majesty during the summer break at Balmoral. They usually manage to do this all in a single day as the travel arrangements are made for them by the Palace. The routine is that they fly to Aberdeen where

It is not very often that The Queen is seen in trousers, but even here, when she was on a photographic safari, she retained her sense of style with an elegant silk jacket and designer sunglasses. (Jayne Fincher/ © Photographers International)

they are met by one of the Royal cars and a footman whose job is to help carry the bags. Arriving at Balmoral, they are offered lunch and then join The Queen in her sitting room on the first floor where the fitting is to take place. Everything has been planned down to the last detail, and once the session is over and both The Queen and the designer are satisfied, he or she is then driven back to Aberdeen to catch a commercial flight to London. Seats have been reserved and British Airways notified of the identity of the passengers, so if there is a slight delay on the road through heavy traffic or some other hold-up, the aircraft will wait as long as the delay is not too long. The designers enjoy going up to Balmoral; it's a break with normal daily routine and there's usually an additional bonus. Before they leave they are always given a parcel of Balmoral produce: game, fish or haggis.

The Queen enjoys wearing knitted sweaters and woollen skirts. The sweaters are made for her by Pringle of Scotland Ltd at their factory in the Borders at Hawick. The company was founded in 1815 and have held a warrant from The Queen since 1956. They also supply pure cashmere socks to the Princess Royal.

The Royal Family likes to patronise the local shops in Ballater, the town nearest to Balmoral Castle. One of them, Henderson's, supplies The Queen with some of the outfits she wears in the Highlands, including kilts and tweed skirts. Not many people have seen Her Majesty wearing trousers. They are not her favourite garment but those she does wear are made for her by her tailor, Peter Enricone, who favours classical lines that flatter the figure.

If the late Diana, Princess of Wales was described as the saviour of the British fashion industry and, in particular, the millinery side, then The Queen also has a branch of fashion that has special reason to be grateful to her. She is rarely seen in public without a pair of gloves. She can wear up to five pairs in a single day and they are made for her by Cornelia James of Brighton. Mrs James started out making gloves for Norman Hartnell and Hardy Amies in the 1950s. This, of course, was a time when no self-respecting lady would dream of being seen without gloves, but the fashion gradually began to die out until The Queen made them fashionable again. She is without doubt the company's best individual customer and, albeit unwittingly, its best advertisement also.

If there is one area where The Queen and her daughter, Anne, disagree it is over shoes. Princess Anne hates to spend money on expensive shoes;

The Queen, who regularly spends hours on her feet, knows that cheap shoes are a false economy – not that cost is a priority. Her footwear has to be comfortable and, if not stylish, at least elegant. But such comfort comes at a price. Her everyday shoes start at around £500, while for some of the diamond-studded evening shoes she wears at State Banquets, she wouldn't get much change out of £5,000.

The Queen's dresses can cost thousands of pounds, with £2,000 being the norm for an evening gown if it does not contain too many jewels. The cost of the Royal wardrobe is met mainly by the Privy Purse, to whom the invoices are sent, after suitable discounts are negotiated. However, if The Queen is going abroad on a State Visit, the entire cost of her wardrobe is met by the Foreign Office.

Maureen Rose made a spectacular full-length gown for Her Majesty to wear during Jubilee Year when almost all foreign royalty were invited to a banquet at Windsor Castle. The embroidered ivory dress involved four seamstresses working full-time for 600 hours and when Maureen Rose retired at the end of 2004, The Queen gave her a signed photograph of herself wearing the dress. It is a proud boast of Maureen Rose that 'no dress we made for The Queen ever saw a machine. Every one was hand-finished.'

Another thing all the designers had to be aware of when they were making clothes for The Queen was the accessories she would be wearing. Therefore Her Majesty would often send her senior dresser, Angela Kelly, to fetch a particular necklace or pair of earrings, which she would then put on – with the unfinished garment – so the designer could see where the neckline should be.

The various couturiers naturally had different views about which colours best suited The Queen. But they all agreed that daffodil yellow was brilliant in bringing out the 'whole being' of Her Majesty, while periwinkle blue matched the colour of her eyes, particularly at night. Maureen Rose had only one reservation about colour and that was mulberry or wine. When she was still working for Ian Thomas she was forced to make a dress in that colour, which she hated, saying it didn't flatter The Queen at all. In fact, it was the only thing that made her look 'frumpy'.

Recently, Her Majesty has installed a workroom at Buckingham Palace, under the strict supervision of Angela Kelly, where some clothes are now made 'in house'. Miss Kelly also advises on designs that are then sent to one of the established dressmakers when necessary. So far, the success of this latest cost-cutting venture has yet to be revealed.

Royal Style

One of the perks of being appointed to be a lady-in-waiting to The Queen is that they also become clients of her dress designers, some with more grace than others. Lady Susan Hussey and Diana, Lady Farnham, are two for whom the designers love to make. They never cause difficulties and often ease the path when they are summoned to the Palace.

In the early days of The Queen's reign there was a staidness about the outfits worn by everyone at Court, both male and female. It wasn't quite as formal as when Her Majesty's grandfather, King George V, was on the throne, for he wore a tail coat and the Garter, while his wife, Queen Mary, wore full-length gowns complete with tiara, every night at dinner, even when they were dining alone. The Queen and Prince Philip didn't go quite that far. But they did dress for dinner during the first decade of her reign. These days, they are far more relaxed and informal. The Queen wears short day dresses in the evening if they are at home, while Prince Philip changes from his usual daytime lounge suit into a sports coat and casual trousers – all beautifully pressed by one of his two valets, of course.

For most daytime engagements, The Queen wears a hat. If the function takes place in the early evening, such as the Chelsea Flower Show – a hardy annual – a hat is not usually worn as she regards these events as less formal. Currently, her favoured milliners are Philip Somerville and Marie O'Regan. Her Majesty always wears clothes made for her by British designers and apart from those mentioned above, she also uses the talents of Stewart Parvin, who is based in London.

If The Queen could be said to have retained her own style throughout the fifty-odd years she has been on the throne, it shows how successful she has been. If she had tried to become more contemporary it wouldn't have worked. In all things, on all occasions, she has to look like the lady she is. And fashion being what it is, styles appear to have caught up with her, rather than the other way around. Today, pop stars and show-business personalities pay many thousands of pounds and dollars trying to achieve the elegance The Queen has displayed for decades. Fashion inevitably comes full circle, and it is to The Queen's advantage that it has done so once again. In her eightieth year her dress, deportment and manners reflect standards that have in the main all but disappeared from practically every class and generation, but if she is not everyone's idea of a fashion plate, at least she knows what suits her.

The Queen and the *Commonwealth*

T he Queen has never had to subject herself to the indignity of an election – though one prominent American citizen once asked Princess Anne, during a visit to the United States, to 'congratulate your mother on being re-elected'. But if Her Majesty had been asked to stand for the one position she holds, not through right of birth, as Head of the Commonwealth, she would, no doubt, have been returned unopposed.

It is difficult for most people in Britain to recognise the importance The Queen places on her role in the Commonwealth. British people tend to think of her as 'The Queen' and nothing else. But to the 1 billion men, women and children who populate those countries in what was once the British Empire, The Queen is regarded as someone who is far above mere politics. To them she is a link with the past and a reminder of the special relationship they each have with the United Kingdom – the mother country.

The Commonwealth is a voluntary organisation made up of independent sovereign states that were formerly part of the British Empire – with one exception. That is Mozambique, a one-time Portuguese colony, which asked to join the Commonwealth in 1995.

There is no compulsion for former colonies to join the Commonwealth; it is entirely voluntary. Eire was once a member but resigned in 1949 on

The Queen shares a toast with the Secretary-General of the Commonwealth, Don McKinnon at a dinner held for Commonwealth Heads of Government in Abuja, Nigeria in 2003. (Kirsty Wigglesworth/PA/EMPICS)

becoming the Irish Republic, and South Africa, which was one of the original members in 1847, along with Australia, New Zealand and Canada, left in 1961, owing to worldwide criticism of its apartheid policies, and then applied to be readmitted in 1994, following the success of the election that saw Nelson Mandela becoming the country's first black president, and the end of apartheid. The importance placed on membership of the Commonwealth was emphasised by President Mandela as his application to rejoin was among the first actions he took after being elected to office.

Five former colonies declined to join when they became independent: Burma, British Somaliland, Cameroon, the Republic of the Maldives and Aden, which became the Yemen. And one, Zimbabwe, is suspended from the Commonwealth at the time of writing.

Most of the countries of the Commonwealth do not recognise The Queen as their Head of State. Indeed, four of them – Lesotho, Malaysia, Swaziland and Tonga – have their own monarchies, while Western Samoa has a Paramount Chief. The majority of the others are republics with an elected president as their Head of State. But all of these countries in the Commonwealth have acclaimed The Queen as Head of the Commonwealth.

In each of those realms that do recognise The Queen as Head of State, she possesses exactly the same function as she does in the United

Kingdom. She is head of the legislature, the executive and the judiciary, and all legal and government business is enacted in her name, with the formal actions being carried out on her behalf by a governor-general who is her personal representative, though she plays no part in selecting them. The candidate is chosen by the government of the country concerned and The Queen appoints him or her on the recommendation of the prime minister of that country.

As Head of the Commonwealth, Her Majesty enjoys tremendous prestige and influence but the title is purely symbolic, carrying with it no constitutional authority. And she distinguishes between her different roles – Head of State in some countries and Queen of the United Kingdom in those member countries that are republics – by flying a different personal flag. Where the Royal Standard is considered inappropriate she uses a flag with the initial 'E' and a crown within a chaplet of roses. Her Majesty is sensitive to the feelings of all the members of the Commonwealth and regards such details as important.

As a stateswoman The Queen plays a vital part in the administrative affairs of the Commonwealth and she has achieved several 'firsts' in her role. She is the first British Sovereign to have opened the Parliaments of Australia, New Zealand, Canada and Sri Lanka (then Ceylon). When she spoke from the throne at the Opening of the Parliament of Canada in 1957, she said: 'I greet you as your Queen. Together we constitute the Parliament of Canada . . .'

The Commonwealth organisation's headquarters is in London, in a grand house provided for it by The Queen. It is Marlborough House in Pall Mall, the home of Her Majesty's grandmother, Queen Mary, after the death of George V in 1936, and the room where the Commonwealth Secretary-General, Don McKinnon, now has his office was the bedroom where the old queen died in 1953. The Secretary-General is the chief executive of the Commonwealth. A tall, athletic-looking New Zealander, Don McKinnon is remarkably unstuffy for someone who occupies such an important and unique position. A former chief whip and foreign secretary in his own country, he brought a wealth of experience to the job, having known most of the leaders of the Commonwealth for many years. He was appointed at a Commonwealth Conference in Durban, South Africa in 1999 but he had already met The Queen some years before.

It was during a Royal visit to New Zealand and my first impression of her was that she had a fantastic smile. It was absolute naturalness and I thought, 'Why can't the rest of the world see her like this?' Up until then I had just seen TV clips and still photographs, none of which do her justice. Then when I was given the job, she came up to me and said she hoped I would enjoy coming to London and that made me feel pretty welcome, because, knowing her role was essentially a titular one, I felt her words were sincere.

But how difficult is it for a republic within the Commonwealth to accept The Queen as its Head? Mr McKinnon explains the background to the decision.

It all goes back to 1953 when there were just eight members of the organisation – as compared to fifty-three today – and Pandit Nehru, India's leader, persuaded the others to acknowledge The Queen as Head. And, as others have joined they have all accepted her in the same way because she has been in her job longer than anyone else in the Commonwealth has been in his or hers. She has known their predecessors and their predecessors' predecessors. This is what gives her that special authority and she has a prodigious memory, she can recall names and events of decades ago, so at the present time it suits everyone to have her as titular Head. But the position is not automatically given to the British Sovereign and Commonwealth leaders are obviously going to have to address this issue at some time in the future. All the leaders know The Queen personally, they do not know the Prince of Wales in the same way, so there may be pause for thought.

The Secretary-General enjoys a special relationship with The Queen. He is not required to go through the Prime Minister's Office – or any other government department – in his dealings with Buckingham Palace.

I would feel it would be an absolute insult if I had to go through Number Ten. I have direct access to The Queen and when we meet it is only the two of us in the room. There are no private secretaries, the agenda is completely informal and we talk about anything and everything under the sun. No notes are taken, but The Queen has obviously done her

Her Majesty attends all Commonwealth Summit Conferences and here she addresses the opening session in Nigeria in December 2003. It was a particularly controversial meeting as Zimbabwe had been expelled, and there was a split between western countries and African members about Robert Mugabe's readmittance. The summit opened without Zimbabwe. (PA/EMPICS)

homework and she raises all sorts of issues. She always wants to be kept fully up to date with the family. By that I mean the Commonwealth family. She has an intense interest in all things to do with the organisation even though she takes no active part in the business meetings at our Conferences. I think it is important that she is not involved in that side of the organisation; it keeps her above politics. One great advantage in having The Queen as Head of the organisation is that all the leaders of all the member countries have tremendous respect for her and a lot of admiration and affection. They know they can share a joke with her, ask her anything and they guard jealously the right they have to have a private audience of her at the Commonwealth Conferences. I think she regards this tradition as equally important and she makes sure she sees every one of them individually. Of course, there are a number of countries that may disagree violently with the British Government's point of view, often blaming Britain for the ills that may have befallen them since independence. It doesn't necessarily mean they also disagree with what The Queen is saying. Anyway, she is brilliant in avoiding controversial issues.

As a titular symbol of the former power that ruled them from thousands of miles away, she might have been the subject of personal abuse, but so far this has never happened.

There have been attempts on occasion to bring her into the front line of politics, but they have all failed, as Don McKinnon remembers, 'Margaret Thatcher tried to politicise her by saying "you should not go to Lusaka [in 1979], to the Heads of Government Meeting", but The Queen refused to be drawn into this particular row, and she went.'

At this specific conference, the African countries without exception were extremely hostile to Margaret Thatcher, thinking she did not believe in black majority rule. It was one of the most dangerous moments for the Commonwealth but, as Lord Carrington, at that time Britain's Foreign and Commonwealth Secretary, recalls:

It was a great eye-opener to see the way The Queen dealt with this. She saw each one of the Heads of Government individually, for exactly the same amount of time – and don't ask me how that was worked out – and they all melted. From that moment on the whole atmosphere of the conference changed. It was very interesting to see the effect her efforts had. Her secret was – and remains – that she treats everybody the same. There's no preference for Britain, and that came as a very pleasant surprise to some of the other members.

In the fifty-four years The Queen has been on the throne – and Head of the Commonwealth – she has travelled more than any other monarch the world has ever known. She has been to every country in the Commonwealth, some several times, and to almost every other country on earth. So this must give her a breadth of experience denied to any other statesman in the world. It would be understandable if one supposed that her sympathies lay mainly with the 'white' countries of the 'old' Dominions: Canada, Australia, New Zealand and South Africa. The newer African, Asian and West Indian former colonies have always been slightly suspicious of the fact that the Commonwealth Secretariat is housed in a former home of a British Queen, perhaps too close to the heart of what was once a mighty imperialist empire. But the Secretary-General puts paid to that particular myth.

The Queen is colour blind when it comes to dealing with leaders from Africa, the Caribbean or Asia. It makes no difference at all to the way she talks with them. She chats as if she is among old friends, which, in most cases, she is. After more than half a century of travelling around the globe she is very familiar with all the countries in the Commonwealth and she treats them all the same, unlike some other world leaders. Let's face it; she's seen it all. There's nothing new they can tell her.

So, as Kenneth Kaunda, President of Zambia from 1964 to 1991, once remarked to the author, 'She is the cement that holds the Commonwealth together.' But belonging to the same family of nations has not always meant peaceful relations between its members. India and Pakistan were at war with each while both remained part of the Commonwealth, and a number of African countries have found their armies fighting each other in border disputes.

The Queen once said that the original aim of the Commonwealth was 'to make an effective contribution towards redressing the economic balance between nations'. Presumably what she meant by those words was to bring

The Queen and the Duke of Edinburgh with fifteen Governors-General of the Commonwealth at their first ever joint meeting at Windsor Castle. It was the first public duty for The Queen following the death of her mother in April 2002. (Fiona Hanson/PA/EMPICS)

up the standard of living of her people in the poorer black and Asian countries, to that enjoyed by those in Britain, Australia, New Zealand and Canada. It hasn't happened. In many cases the standard of living in the poorer countries has dropped drastically since they gained their independence.

After fifty-four years, what does Don McKinnon think are the main strengths of The Queen regarding the Commonwealth?

> Simply by being there, by representing some very core solid and relevant values. She knows what is good about the various civilisations around the world and the fact that she has a very strong faith herself. Now even if you are not a Christian, you can understand her faith is important to her and part of her very being. Added to which, three of her four children have been divorced so she knows what life is like. Even for someone like her, who most people think is protected from the normal everyday problems that affect families, it must have had an effect. No parent can go through that kind of drama without it having some sort of effect, so emotionally she's been knocked about a bit. And when that happens you either stay fallen or you stand up a lot stronger and you know she has come through these things – she's had to.

Kenneth Kaunda summed up the feelings of his fellow members of the Commonwealth when he said, 'Without her as mother, this family of nations would have divided years ago. And remember, we are not members just by accident of colonial history but by conviction.'

Many Commonwealth leaders have become personal friends of The Queen in spite of their countries having different political views from Britain. Lee Kwan Yew, Minister Mentor of Singapore, and the island state's first Prime Minister, first met The Queen in 1966 and was immediately impressed at how she put him and everyone she met at ease. As he put it, 'It was a social skill perfected by years of training and experience.' Harry Lee – as he is known to his fellow Commonwealth leaders – is also one of the few political figures to have heard The Queen express what could be termed a political opinion. It was in January 1969 when they met in London: 'She said she was sorry the British had decided to withdraw from Singapore.' The remark was made in private and would not have been universally welcomed in Singapore itself, but Lee Kwan Yew knew she was speaking only out of affection for his country, not because of the loss of part of the British Empire.

The Queen bestowed several honours on Singapore's first Prime Minister, including making him a Companion of Honour (CH) in the 1970 New Year's Honours List, and then in 1972 during her visit to Singapore she made him a Knight Grand Cross of the Order of St Michael and St George (GCMG). However, he did not use the title 'Sir' that automatically went with the GCMG: 'I did not think it appropriate . . . but I was pleased and proud to have received two coveted British trophies . . .'.

No insult was intended in not using the title; many prominent people who are citizens of foreign countries and who have received honours from The Queen, decline to use the titles that accompany them. Dr Henry Kissinger, the distinguished former United States statesman, was given an honorary knighthood, which he cherishes to this day, but in America it would be totally inappropriate for him to use the prefix 'Sir'. The same applied to the late Douglas Fairbanks Jr. who was knighted by The Queen's father after his gallant services to Britain during the Second World War. He didn't call himself 'Sir Douglas' but he didn't object if someone else did on occasion.

Lord (David) Owen is a former Foreign and Commonwealth Secretary who held the post in the Labour Government from 1977 to 1979. He recalled The Queen's skill at dealing with some long-serving African leaders who had experienced problems with Britain. 'I saw that she could and did say things which would have been impossible for me as Foreign Secretary to say. I would soon have been told it was none of my business, but she could get away with it without anyone taking umbrage. They had a respect for her judgement and also for her as a person . . . she gave the completely correct impression that the Commonwealth matters to her personally.'

The Queen's principal role at Commonwealth conferences is to make herself available to any and all the member countries' leaders should they want to discuss any matter in private and in total confidence. Several members have indicated that the organisation would not be the same if she were not there. She gives the Commonwealth a dignity and status it would be difficult to sustain without her presence. Britain likes to think of itself as

Even in the warmest weather The Queen remains cool, calm and collected. Here, in the baking heat of Nigeria, she wears gloves and a hat as she is greeted by crowds of respectful wellwishers as she carries out one of her now obligatory 'walkabouts'. (Jayne Fincher/© Photographers International)

being at the heart of the Commonwealth and in many ways, its leader. It is not. The nostalgic feeling is simply a throwback to the old days of the British Empire that disappeared for good decades ago. Today, Britain is just another member of this unique organisation and to the other member states The Queen's role as their Head is much more important than her position as Britain's Head of State. So when she eventually goes – and every Commonwealth leader hopes that will not be for many years to come – her successor as Head of the Commonwealth will not necessarily be the heir to the throne.

The Prince of Wales does not enjoy anywhere near the same level of respect and affection as his mother. His marital problems and the fact that when he remarried it was to a divorced woman whose first husband is still living, cause great discomfort and unease in several Commonwealth countries particularly in those religious African countries, where the sanctity of marriage is still held in high regard. Prince Charles is going to have to work hard to convince all fifty-three member states that he is the right man for the job. There is a well of goodwill for the Royal Family, but The Queen's only daughter, the Princess Royal, who has made many visits to Commonwealth countries as President of the Save the Children Fund, could well be the front runner if it comes to an election in due course. In several African and Asian countries she is second in popularity only to The Queen and even though she, too, is divorced and married for the second time, no stigma appears to have been attached to her. Her workload is the highest in the Royal Family and her sense of duty unchallenged. In addition she has been recognised internationally when she was nominated for the Nobel Peace Prize in 1990 and in a distinguished field was narrowly beaten by the then Soviet leader, Mikhail Gorbachev. Her nomination was enthusiastically supported by two Commonwealth leaders, Presidents Kenneth Kaunda of Zambia and Robert Mugabe of Zimbabwe.

When The Queen was crowned as Elizabeth II in 1953 she was presented with a magnificent trophy, the Commonwealth Vase. Standing 24in high and weighing 29lb, the ten-sided vase is surmounted with a crown, while its centre panel is made up of the Royal Coat of Arms. The panels surrounding it contain the symbols of the United Kingdom and the emblems of those countries that were members of the Commonwealth at that time. This constant reminder to The Queen of her most important role is kept at the Palace of Holyroodhouse in Edinburgh. Not that she needs anything to remind her of her place in this family of nations. To her, there is virtually no difference in her roles as Queen of the United Kingdom and Head of the Commonwealth. She treats each with the same amount of respect and devotion.

A former Secretary-General of the Commonwealth, Sir Sonny Ramphal, said the reason why The Queen has been so widely accepted as Head of the Commonwealth is because she has demonstrated to all the member countries that she genuinely cares about them. Which was something not all expected from post-imperial Britain, and which has been the key to her unquestioned success in the Commonwealth.

The World's Most
Experienced
Stateswoman

To watch The Queen with other world leaders is to witness a master class in international diplomacy. She invariably seems to know the right things to say, and the correct time to say them, without ever giving offence, or offering a clue as to her own opinions. Her Majesty gives the appearance of being able to talk off the cuff on any subject to men and women who have been involved in some of the world's most difficult problems in the last half-century. But her outwardly calm demeanour disguises the fact that she will have spent hours being briefed and doing her homework before the meetings. The Queen is a fervent believer in being totally prepared for every eventuality. She is far and away the most experienced stateswoman in the world – and it shows. When she speaks to President George W. Bush, the most powerful man on earth, she is able to remind him of similar subjects she discussed with his father ten years earlier when he was President of the United States.

Her role as Head of State of the United Kingdom has taken her to nearly every country in the world and the longer she has been on the throne the more she has matured into the matriarchal figure she has now become. There is nothing patronising about her approach to the leaders of other countries, many of whom were not even born when she became Queen. But her personal experience of some of the problems they have encountered has given her a wisdom they all respect and admire. The fact that she is non-political and does not represent or have to conform to any particular party line elevates her to a status they can only dream of.

She is as comfortable with Presidents such as Lech Walesa, the one-time Polish Head of State, a former miner who was born in a two-up, two-down cottage and to whom Buckingham Palace must have seemed like an alien planet, as she was with old friends of her father, like President Eisenhower, whom she visited at the White House in 1957 and who had been a guest at Balmoral. The Queen had known President Eisenhower since the Second World War when, as General Eisenhower, he became friendly with George VI, so their relationship went beyond that of just two Heads of State. In fact, the President insisted that The Queen and Prince Philip should stay at the White House and not in Blair House, the official guest house for visiting Heads of State. Her Majesty was given the Rose Room while Prince Philip was intrigued to occupy the Lincoln Room which still contained Abraham Lincoln's four-poster bed. It was just prior to that State Visit to the United States in 1957 that the *Washington Post*, arguably America's most influential newspaper, said: 'This country accords Her Majesty no title, but it offers her, we think, its heart.'

Since those words were written, every American President has welcomed The Queen and she has become friends with them all, Republican and Democrat alike. Gerald Ford told me that he could not believe he was 'dancing with The Queen of England at the White House', while Bill Clinton said his evening on the Royal Yacht *Britannia*, and lunch the following day with the Queen Mother and Princess Diana, was an experience never to be forgotten.

It was in June 1994 that President Clinton and his wife Hillary came to Britain to celebrate the fiftieth anniversary of the D-Day landings. At a dinner in Portsmouth, the President was seated next to The Queen and in his book *My Life* published in 2004, he said he was taken with her grace and intelligence and the clever manner in which she discussed public issues, probing for information and insights without venturing too far into expressing her own political views. President Clinton added, 'Her Majesty impressed me as someone who, but for the circumstances of her birth, might have become a successful politician or diplomat. As it was, she had to be both, without quite seeming to be either.'

The Queen was joined onboard the Royal Yacht Britannia by many Heads of State and their wives to commemorate the fiftieth anniversary of the D-Day Landings. In the front row from left to right are: Mrs Norma Major, President Lech Walesa of Poland, HM King Harald of Norway, President Bill Clinton, The Queen, the Duke of Edinburgh, Mrs Hillary Clinton, Prince Bernard of The Netherlands and Prime Minister John Major. (Martin Keene/PA/EMPICS)

President George W. Bush and his wife Laura enjoyed their visit to Buckingham Palace and later the President said his conversations with Her Majesty kept him on his toes.

President Ronald Reagan said the two women, apart from his wife, that he admired above all others were The Queen and Margaret Thatcher. The Queen gave President and Mrs Reagan a wedding anniversary party on board *Britannia* in San Diego and later he said, after seeing the march past by the band of the Royal Marines, arranged for them specially by The Queen, 'I come from Hollywood, the entertainment capital of the world, but I don't think we could beat this.'

In 1955, just three years into The Queen's reign, the Central Office of Information issued a pamphlet, which stated: 'In law, the Sovereign is the only person with authority to represent any part of her dominions in intercourse with a foreign State, and to contract international obligations . . .'.

When she visited Canada in May 2005 (which was not described as a State Visit, but as a 'stay' because she is, of course, Queen of Canada), where the large French-speaking part of the population has been vociferous in its criticism of the monarchy and where there is great enthusiasm for the country to become a republic, she won over everyone with her realistic approach. Speaking to 1,200 guests at the official Government of Canada banquet, she said: 'Of course the relationship between Crown and Canada evolves with the times, as it should . . . but I for one can sense the continuity. It seems to me like yesterday that small girls offered me flowers on my first visit fifty-four years ago, yet today, I suspect, it is their grandchildren who are presenting the bouquets.'

Her Majesty spoke in English and near impeccable French, to the delight of her hosts. She also underlined the importance of Canada to the Crown and how vital it was to her personally that the relationship should continue. Addressing the Alberta Legislature, she said: 'During a previous visit thirty-two years ago, I said: "I want the Crown in Canada to represent everything that is

The Queen arriving in Regina, Canada at the start of her visit to Saskatchewan and Alberta in May 2005. Her Majesty was welcomed by Cree Chief, Alphonse Bird, in traditional Indian headdress at the First Nations University. (Ian Jones/Daily Telegraph/PA/EMPICS)

One way to guarantee attracting The Queen's attention is to show up with some of her favourite breed of dog. As she leaves the Alberta Legislature in Canada, Her Majesty stops to meet a group of corgis. (Paul Chiasson/Canada Press/ EMPICS)

best and most admired in the Canadian ideal. I will continue to do my best to make it so during my lifetime, and I hope you will all continue to give me your help in this task."' She added: 'I would like to repeat those words today as, together, we continue to build a country that remains the envy of the world.' It was a brilliant example of The Queen of Canada addressing her people and showing them that she was not some visiting potentate, but their Queen sharing their problems and aspirations.

Her command of the French language has also helped paper over the cracks in relationships between Britain and France on at least one significant occasion. In April 1960, a spectacular State Visit to Britain was arranged for the French President Charles de Gaulle. As the wartime leader of the Free French in London, General de Gaulle had frequently crossed swords with the then British Prime Minister Winston Churchill. Each thought the other to be arrogant and pig-headed (which was probably true in both cases), and after the war de Gaulle could barely speak to Churchill.

On the occasion of this State Visit, the President, who had been greatly supported and quietly but firmly encouraged during the Second World War by The Queen's father, King George VI, spoke movingly of his affection for the Royal Family. Addressing The Queen during a State Banquet in his honour, he said, 'Where else, Madame, better than in your presence could I bear witness to my gratitude?' It was a case where The Queen, with her charm and innate good manners, had soothed the feelings of the President, even though three years later he obstructed Britain's attempts to join the European Community by using his veto. In retaliation, the government then cancelled a proposed visit to France by Princess Margaret. There was a 'diplomatic excuse' offered in that Her Royal Highness, as a Counsellor of State, could not leave Britain at that time. It was all rubbish, of course, as the visit had been arranged months before in the full knowledge of the Princess's and The Queen's diaries.

Britain and the Vatican are regarded as the two most stable states in the world and the heads of these states are held in equally high regard. The Queen enjoyed a particular affinity with the late Pope John Paul II, who died in 2005. Her Majesty paid two State Visits to Italy during which she twice met the Pope and in return he was welcomed to Buckingham Palace.

In October 2000, The Queen realised His Holiness was in poor health: his hearing was failing and his sight was causing great concern. Her Majesty spoke a little louder than usual during her visit and she walked at his slow pace rather than her own. The two religious leaders – the Pope as Head of the Roman Catholic Church on earth and The Queen as Supreme Governor of the Church of England – found they had much in common, including a mutual interest in ancient sacred documents, and the Pope was delighted to discover that The Queen was not merely being polite but showed an expertise he had not expected.

In her years on the throne, The Queen has developed a particular understanding of the art of human relationships. One example of this is the manner in which she treats members of other European royalty who have been exiled as their countries have become republics. King Constantine of The Helenes, who has lived in London since being deposed as King of Greece, has been shown great compassion by The Queen. She enjoys his company and he is a frequent guest at British Royal functions where he is always referred to as His Majesty.

The State Visits made by The Queen in the last half-century have been magnificent and memorable, friendly and, on some occasions, hilarious. On one visit to Portugal, Her Majesty and Prince Philip rejected the Rolls-Royce limousine that accompanies them wherever they go. Instead, they opted to travel on top of an open-topped bus, causing great amusement and a huge, spontaneous outpouring of affection from an adoring crowd of onlookers.

In the United States, The Queen was asked what she would most like to see. She replied that an American football game was one thing about which

Her Majesty welcomed President George W. Bush to Buckingham Palace at the beginning of his four-day visit to Britain in November 2003. A State Banquet was held in his honour and here The Queen is seen wearing the family honours on her left shoulder. (PA/EMPICS)

she had heard plenty but knew nothing, so she was invited to watch a match between the Universities of Maryland and North Carolina. Her reaction to this most intricate and complicated of sporting activities has never been recorded.

One essential part of a State Visit is the exchange of gifts between the two Heads of State. The Queen has received presents worth millions of pounds from her hosts: jewels, diamonds, gold, priceless carpets and, on one occasion, a baby crocodile that had to be kept in her Private Secretary's bath. She usually gives her hosts a signed, framed photograph of herself with Prince Philip. The photograph is of little intrinsic value and might seem a rather poor return for some of the gifts she has received, but the feeling in the Royal Household is that as most of the recipients have just about everything they could want anyway, this very personal gift is an ideal way for The Queen to show her appreciation. Indeed, one of the rulers of an oil-rich Middle Eastern state, who once gave her presents valued at over £2 million, was overjoyed when he received his signed photograph in a solid silver frame.

The Queen also keeps a detailed record of everything she has been given and by whom, so that if that person later visits Buckingham Palace or Windsor Castle, he or she will find their gift displayed prominently – even if it has been stored somewhere else for years.

When President George Bush Sr. came to tea with The Queen some years after leaving office, he noticed an unusual three-legged silver dish on a table. He asked The Queen what it was. Her Majesty replied, with a smile, 'I thought you would be able to tell me. You gave it to me.' The President later told me that he had a Head of Protocol who would have chosen the gift, '. . . but I still should have known'.

The Queen's undoubted skills as a diplomat have been called on many times. She has been forced to act as hostess to the leaders of several countries with whom Britain has been at war. In 1969, Emperor Hirohito of Japan was invited to visit Britain. The government was anxious to attract Japanese investment and a State Visit was thought to be one way of persuading Japanese companies to put money into this country. But there were still many people in Britain who remembered the appalling atrocities committed by Japan against British and Allied men, women and children during the Second World War. Thousands objected to the visit and when The Queen and the Emperor drove down The Mall towards Buckingham Palace in an open carriage, the shouted insults at the Emperor were plainly heard by everyone in the procession. The Queen managed to keep smiling and later she was heard to say that she was glad the Emperor didn't understand a word of English.

Before the war Emperor Hirohito had been made an honorary Knight of the Garter, and when Japan entered the conflict against Britain, King George VI ordered his shield to be removed from St George's Hall. It was during the 1969 visit that the shield was replaced. The visit also caused The Queen to be placed in an embarrassing situation with Earl Mountbatten of Burma, Prince Philip's uncle. Mountbatten had received the surrender of the Japanese in Singapore in 1945, but he had been horrified at the condition of the prisoners he released and he never forgave the Japanese.

So he absented himself from the State Banquet for Emperor Hirohito claiming, in order to spare The Queen's feelings, a 'previous engagement'.

Perhaps the most delicate State Visit The Queen has undertaken was that to Germany in 1965. It had taken years to arrange, partly because of the persisent anti-German feelings in Britain, twenty years after the end of the Second World War. Both The Queen and Prince Philip have strong German connections through their joint ancestors and it was feared in Britain that much would be made of Her Majesty's German blood, thereby stirring up anti-monarchist feelings in the country.

The Queen was also ambivalent in her emotions. She had spent the formative years of her life in a Britain at war with Germany, and her mother never tried to hide her dislike for the people who had bombed Buckingham Palace and the East End of London. And even though the German President had been on a State Visit to Britain in 1958, his reception had been cool to say the least. So for The Queen, it was a journey into uncharted territory, and one she was not guaranteed to enjoy.

Prince Philip was not at all put out at the thought of visiting Germany, and looked forward to meeting members of his family, but he was aware of the problems that might arise, particularly with protocol. Which of his relations should be invited to the formal functions and where should they be seated in what was now a democracy? Some members of his family had been Nazi sympathisers so obviously they could not be included, while The Queen's distant relations mostly lived in what was then East Germany and it would be difficult for them to travel to the west.

Eventually all the problems were solved and The Queen said she had enjoyed the visit, but it must have tested her diplomatic skills severely, and much to the relief of the Royal Household and the then British Ambassador, the British media did not emphasise her German family connections as strongly as they might have done. Prince Philip had, moreover, an opportunity to use his German, for he is fluent in the language, while The Queen doesn't speak a word. But this has frequently been the case in other countries she has visited. She has been forced to listen to endless speeches in a language she doesn't understand and appear to give her undivided attention to the speaker. On one occasion when she was replying, it seemed as if Prince Philip had fallen asleep through boredom. When he was asked later if that had been the case, he replied: 'No. It was during the President's speech.'

In May 1991, during a State Visit to the United States, as the guest of President George Bush Sr., The Queen became the first British monarch to address a joint meeting of Congress in Washington DC. (© Anwar Hussein)

Lord Carrington held several Cabinet posts that brought him into contact with The Queen. As a former Foreign and Commonwealth Secretary, he accompanied her on a number of overseas tours and he is unequivocal in his praise and admiration. 'She has an aura about her, a glamour that republics and even some kingdoms don't have. Her demeanour has an extraordinary effect when she is abroad that is reflected in people's perception of Britain as a whole.' Lord (David) Owen, another former Foreign Secretary, says, 'The Queen calls on reserves within all of us. We go that little extra mile for her.'

Generations of British politicians have liked to claim there is a special relationship between Britain and the United States – and more than one has boasted that he, or she, has been mainly responsible for maintaining it. The former US Secretary of State, Henry Kissinger, is in no doubt that it is the character and personal qualities of The Queen that have made the most significant single contribution. 'Whenever I see her with American Presidents, I cannot believe she can behave in the same way with every other country. She has made a unique and enormous contribution to US/Anglo relations. There is

The Queen is joined by an old friend, William S. Farish, at that time US Ambassador to the United Kingdom, as they leave St Paul's Cathedral after a service in memory of those killed in the terrorist attacks on the World Trade Centre in New York in September 2001. (Toby Melville/PA/EMPICS)

no doubt in my mind that she is respected and admired here more than any other Head of State.'

Although The Queen is considered to be above politics, many foreign Heads of State discuss world affairs with her during State Visits, and inevitably she reflects the views of her government in Britain and occasionally those of the Commonwealth. When Harold Wilson was Prime Minister, he said that on occasions The Queen knew more about the foreign policy of countries he was dealing with than he did. She would often hint at what he could expect but never give him chapter and verse, and never reveal her sources. He said her assistance was invaluable and he never once betrayed her confidences.

The Queen does not reveal what goes on between her and her ministers or between her and the Heads of State she meets. But in all the years she has been on the throne, she has never been accused of doing anything dishonourable or dishonest despite having to deal with more than one political prima donna. She has become the acceptable face of monarchy at a time when British influence has diminished to a point where it is now barely included in the league table of major world powers.

People still look up to her with respect and admiration, and the older she gets, the more she is greeted with affection and esteem wherever she goes. She was once asked by one of her prime ministers how she managed to maintain such high standards of diplomacy when faced with so many examples of corruption and double-dealing among some of the leaders she is forced to meet. She replied that when one has been doing the job as long as she has one learns to keep a smile on one's face in spite of any inner turmoil. She added, modestly, that when one has been Queen for over half a century, one should be starting to get it right. In Her Majesty's case, there are many who would testify that she has never put a foot wrong.

eleven

Daughter and
Sister

A s Princess Elizabeth, The Queen was brought up in a close family unit and in as normal a manner as was possible under the circumstances of her generation and Royal class. She adored her father and the feeling was mutual. He knew what her eventual role was destined to be and tried to protect her as long as he could from the pomp and protocol that was going to be her way of life from the age of 25.

On the day Elizabeth became Queen, in February 1952, the only close adult family she had, apart from her husband, were her mother and her 22-year-old sister, Margaret. They were the three remaining members of 'The Firm' as King George VI liked to call his immediate family.

The Queen enjoyed a warm, loving relationship with her mother and for half a century the senior telephonist at Buckingham Palace used to connect the two Royal ladies every morning with the same words: 'Your Majesty, I have Her Majesty for you.' The Queen called her mother 'Mummy' even when she, The Queen that is, was in her seventies, and the Queen Mother called her elder daughter 'Lillibet', the name by which she had been known in the family since childhood, when she had had difficulty in pronouncing Elizabeth correctly. Within the Royal Household the Queen Mother was always referred to as Queen Elizabeth to differentiate between her and her elder daughter, who is simply The Queen. And it was never 'The Queen Mum' (a tabloid newspaper invention which the Queen Mother hated).

The two Elizabeths greet each other. The Queen leans forward to kiss her mother, watched by Prince Philip, as they come ashore in Scotland at the start of one of their summer holidays. (Jayne Fincher/© Photographers International)

There is no doubt that the Queen Mother thoroughly enjoyed her position as Queen Consort even though she was said to be furious when Dickie Mountbatten, whom she had never liked anyway, told her that she should go down on her knees every night and say a prayer of thanks to Wallis Simpson. When she coldly demanded to know what he meant he replied, 'Well, without her, we would not have had you.' It was a typically sycophantic remark by a man who never lost a chance to ingratiate himself with the Royal Family, but Queen Elizabeth did not welcome the intended compliment.

She realised the strength of her position and loved being the focus of attention. King George VI was basically a shy man who became a revered monarch to his people, but he was content to allow his wife the limelight. And both daughters, Elizabeth and Margaret, knew that they had to take second place to their mother. She would never have allowed them to become more famous than herself. They knew their place in the family firm. Their mother was the star and they were the supporting players.

It was when the King died in 1952 that overnight the roles of mother and elder daughter were suddenly reversed. No longer would Elizabeth have to take a back seat. She would in future be the centre of attention and her mother was relegated to a position of secondary importance. It was a difficult time for both – and for the courtiers at Buckingham Palace. One remarked at the time that the Queen Mother appeared to ignore the change in her circumstances and tried to continue as if she were still the Queen Consort. Of course, throughout her long life, the Queen Mother had a reputation for ignoring anything unpleasant in the belief that if one disregarded something it would somehow disappear. In later life when she was reported to have amassed a bank overdraft of some £4 million, she declined to reduce her extravagant living conditions and expenses, knowing that the overdraft would be someone else's problem, which of course it became as The Queen settled the account on her mother's behalf.

For both mother and daughter the change could not have been more dramatic. Overnight the position of Queen Consort had vanished and the Queen Mother was no longer the power beside the throne she had been for sixteen years. She was also no more the mistress of Buckingham Palace. In fact, her world had virtually collapsed. Not only did she have to bear the sadness of losing the husband she had cared for for nearly thirty years, now she would have to accept that her daughter was also her Sovereign and – in theory anyway – mother would have to curtsy to her child.

To say that the Queen Mother was jealous of her daughter's new position and power would be to overstate the case, but there were almost certainly moments when she felt she was not receiving quite the attention she deserved. After all, her daughter was getting to grips with being Queen, at the tender age of 25, and as Clarence House, where the Queen Mother would live for the rest of her life, was not ready, she remained living with her daughter and son-in-law at Buckingham Palace. Not the ideal way for a new Sovereign to start her reign, or for a newly widowed former Queen Consort to begin her single life. After five years of living independently with her husband, in Britain and Malta, The Queen now found herself under the same roof as her mother once more – and a mother who found it difficult not to continue as chatelaine of the most famous address in the world.

The Queen went to extraordinary lengths to protect her mother's feelings. She did not insist that the Queen Mother should allow her to precede her when they appeared in public. In a gentle, discreet fashion The Queen made sure they seemed to arrive and depart side by side. Of course, there was a huge reservoir of affection for the Queen Mother. It was only seven years since the end of the Second World War and the people of Britain remembered how she had stood by them in those terrible years. In addition, she had always been a woman whose unique style had drawn attention. She was the first truly glamorous 'star' of the Royal Family and she revelled in a celebrity status that was to continue for the next half-century, until she died at the age of 102.

When she was first widowed, she was only 52 and there were inevitably rumours that she would remarry in due course. The Queen never thought so for a moment. She knew that her father had been the only man in her mother's life and even though she liked to flirt with a number of men, it was all harmless fun and she was never interested in settling down with anyone. James Callaghan said her flirting was part of her charm: 'She had a permanent twinkle in her eye that made you feel you were rather special.'

In those first months of The Queen's reign, the domestic life of the family barely changed at all. The Queen deferred to her mother just as she had for the first twenty-five years of her life. She knew how difficult it was going to be for her mother to adjust and she insisted that she take precedence at private family dinner parties at Buckingham Palace, Windsor and at Sandringham. The Queen Mother appeared to take it as her right anyway, but gradually as the shock of losing her husband wore off, she accepted the fact that her daughter Elizabeth must take precedence and that she now had to adapt to a new role. An important aspect of their new relationship was that the daughter never attempted to compete. The two were mutually supportive and, while the Queen Mother retained her 'star' quality throughout her life, The Queen never even tried to be seen in a similar light.

Once the initial difficulties had been overcome, mother and daughter settled into a warm friendship and loving relationship. The Queen Mother still exerted enormous influence over her daughter in certain areas. When Prince Philip wanted to make some early changes in the Royal Household, The Queen would always say, 'First we should see what Mummy thinks about it', much to his dismay.

The Queen Mother, who, together with her late husband, had been reluctant for Elizabeth to marry Philip, never felt the same affection for him that she did for Tony Armstrong-Jones, later the Earl of Snowdon, her other son-in-law. She kept Philip at arm's length, while Snowdon was always welcome at Clarence House even after his acrimonious divorce from Princess Margaret. It wasn't all Philip's fault. Part of the problem was that he was the nephew of Dickie Mountbatten and since the Abdication crisis of 1936, which saw her husband propelled onto the throne, she had never trusted Mountbatten, who had been Edward VIII's closest friend until the day he gave up the throne, and Mountbatten transferred his loyalty to the new King. So she was naturally suspicious of him and Philip suffered unfairly through the association.

While The Queen deferred to her mother on many subjects, she knew the Queen Mother knew very little about constitutional monarchy and she did not consult her about official matters. During the reign of King George VI, his consort had never been privy to State papers, and when Elizabeth II came to the throne she felt no need to include her mother in the business side of the family firm. Neither did Prince Philip see the contents of the government boxes that followed and still follow The Queen wherever she goes.

The Queen Mother did not feel excluded from this side of her daughter's life; her main problem was that since the end of 1936 she had been the centre of attention, the most sought-after woman in Britain, and the demotion to second place was hard to accept. For the remainder of her life she would occupy a unique position in the life of the nation: a favourite mother, grandmother and eventually great-grandmother.

On the personal side she shared many interests with her elder daughter, the most common being horse racing, though they did not compete against each other. The Queen raced her horses on the flat while the Queen Mother was a successful owner and breeder of National Hunt horses.

Guests who joined the Queen Mother at her weekend home, Royal Lodge in Windsor Great Park, would often find The Queen joining them after church on Sunday morning when, if either lady had had a horse running the previous day, they would be forced to watch a recording of the race, complete with commentary from both Royal owners.

Lord Carrington, a former Foreign Secretary and Defence Secretary to The Queen, was a frequent guest at Royal Lodge and he remembered the great excitement when The Queen would rush into the house on Sunday morning brandishing a video tape of a race that either one of her own or her

Just four years into the reign of Elizabeth II and in this picture of her with her mother and sister, taken at Royal Ascot in 1956, The Queen's horse Alexandra had earlier won the Royal Hunt Cup. The three Royal ladies are all wearing fur as this was long before it became politically incorrect to do so in Britain. [TopFoto.co.uk]

mother's horses had won the day before. Nobody was allowed to speak during the race even though they already knew the result, and the two Royal ladies would then discuss the finer points of the race and of their horses with a knowledge that would astound anyone not familiar with their expertise.

The enthusiasm that mother and daughter shared for racing was not always welcomed by members of either's household. Private Secretaries at

Buckingham Palace and Clarence House sometimes despaired when they were attempting to discuss matters of importance only to find that the respective racing managers were talking with The Queen and the Queen Mother about the next day's prospects. It didn't happen very often but enough occasionally to irritate courtiers who did not always understand their employers' excitement.

Throughout her lifetime, Queen Elizabeth was included in every State occasion. No banquet took place at Buckingham Palace or Windsor Castle without the Queen Mother being placed in a prominent position, and she was always asked by The Queen who she would like to have sitting on either side of her. The Queen Mother was a wonderful conversationalist, but she insisted that her dinner companions should not be boring. There was one former prime minister (said to be the late Sir Edward Heath) who once spent an entire evening answering her questions with monosyllabic replies. He was never seated next to her again. The Queen does not enjoy the same privilege, for as hostess she has to sit next to the guest of honour, whoever he or she might be and no matter how excruciating their company.

The Queen always took a protective attitude towards her younger sister, Princess Margaret, born four years after her. As children they enjoyed each other's company more than most sisters as they were both educated at home and rarely played with other girls beyond the family.

While it is true that a special Buckingham Palace Girl Guide and Brownie Pack was formed to give the princesses a taste of 'ordinary' life, the young girls who were invited to join were all from families well known to the King and Queen and all had grown up surrounded by nannies and housemaids. So, even though not royal, they could hardly be described as from 'ordinary' families. And even within the Palace Guide Pack there was a marked difference in the way in which Elizabeth and Margaret joined in. Elizabeth was never comfortable in the company of the other girls and hated it when they 'camped out' under canvas together. She never liked the thought of being lumped together with outsiders and shrank from undressing in front of her fellow Guides. Margaret, on the other hand, thoroughly enjoyed the experience and threw herself heart and soul into the life of the Brownies and Guides.

Princess Margaret had an entirely different personality from Elizabeth. Where the older girl was the soul of discretion and had an air of dignity even as a youngster, Margaret was extrovert, capricious, naughty and always wanted to be the centre of attention. Margaret was also a

Daughter and Sister

demonstrative child who became an equally outgoing woman. Elizabeth was the exact opposite – and still is. As the younger sister, Margaret was indulged by Elizabeth, and by her parents. In fact, her father spoilt her so much that his courtiers began to dislike her for her arrogance. She was the only person who would arrive late for meals and the King would always forgive her. Everything seemed to come easily to Margaret, whereas Elizabeth tried hard for all she achieved. Her quieter nature and awareness of her future responsibilities, even then, made her more reserved than her sister and when anyone mentioned it, she would laugh it off saying 'Oh, let her get on with it. Everyone loves her. She is so much fun.'

This reservation on the part of Elizabeth was also noticeable in the presence of her mother, another one bubbling with personality. Cecil Beaton once wrote, 'I noticed that, when the Queen was present, her daughter [Elizabeth] made no conversational effort and relapsed into silence.'

Princess Margaret said in later life that not only was Elizabeth her sister, 'She was also my best and really, my only, friend.' She added, 'When she went into the ATS towards the end of the war, she was taught to drive everything from a car to a three-ton lorry. So when she came back to Windsor she taught me to drive. She must have been a pretty good instructor as I learned to handle a car in a week. Even though I was very much under the legal age to drive. But it was only on the private roads around Windsor and Sandringham.'

The beginning of the Second World War in 1939 interrupted a Royal Family holiday at Balmoral, and when the King and Queen hurried back to London they decided to leave their daughters behind in the comparative safety of the Scottish Highlands. Their exile didn't last long and they soon rejoined their parents, until the Blitz began and then they were removed to Sandringham where they saw their mother and father only at weekends. Princess Margaret said some years later that she relied on her older sister totally, 'She could do no wrong in my eyes. She was wonderful. Always patient and never lost her temper with me even when I was as infuriating as only a small girl can be.'

Princess Elizabeth made her first broadcast during the war and at the end she invited Margaret to join her in saying goodnight to the children of the empire. Neither girl was nervous. As Margaret said, 'All we were apprehensive about was coming in at the right moment.'

Both sisters say they grew up rather quickly in the war. So many people they both knew were being sent overseas and quite a few were killed. For

Princess Elizabeth in particular, who was at a more impressionable age, it was a salutary experience.

When Princess Elizabeth joined the ATS her sister was incensed because she was too young at 15. She thought a special dispensation should have been made for her, and Elizabeth had to gently explain the reasons why she couldn't fight for her country, no matter how brave she was. Margaret was having none of it, yelling on one occasion, 'I was born too late.' Part of Margaret's anger was that for the first time, her sister was doing something without her and she hated the idea of being left out.

One of the things Elizabeth and Margaret had in common was a concern for their father when he had to speak in public. King George VI had a stammer that caused him to worry for weeks before a speech, especially if it was to be broadcast. Princess Elizabeth tried hard to help her father but in spite of all her efforts, he never quite mastered the knack of speaking normally in front of a microphone.

Because Elizabeth and Margaret spent so much time together without the company of other young people, Elizabeth was regarded as slightly immature for a young lady on the threshold of womanhood. Margaret was forward, precocious and highly intelligent, but Elizabeth was painfully shy in her youth and it wasn't until she and Prince Philip got together that he was able to prise her out of her shell. She had inherited her shyness from her father, who suffered agonies because of his own father's sternness and the efforts to make him use his right hand when he was naturally left-handed. It was said that this was the reason for the stammer that was never fully cured.

The King tried hard not to treat his daughters differently but inevitably observers noticed that the baby of the family could do no wrong and could get away with anything, no matter how outrageous, while Elizabeth had been brought up with a sense of responsibility from the earliest age. No matter how well meaning her parents were towards both children, Elizabeth was taught about her ultimate future role and always urged to be the quieter of the two. Not that she needed much urging as her natural instinct, then and now, is to be cautious and if that caution has progressed into suspicion, it is a result of her early training.

When the Royal Family returned to live permanently in Buckingham Palace at the end of the war, the King recognised the girls' need to have a modicum of independence, even if that only meant they would be allowed rooms of their own. Prior to this they had always shared a suite. The rooms could scarcely have been more different: Margaret's was decorated in her favourite shade of salmon pink and was littered with a clutter of her personal things: family photographs, manicure sets, writing material and invitations to parties and weddings, while Elizabeth's reflected her tidier mind. Her apartments contained a bedroom with adjoining bathroom, study and sitting room, with a colour scheme of pale pink and fawn and a plain fitted carpet. Her desk, which she would take with her to Clarence House when she married Philip, and which she would later bring back to Buckingham Palace on her accession to the throne, was a model of workmanlike efficiency with everything in its place. And even in those days, her footman was instructed to place a fresh pad of black blotting paper on her desk every morning.

Elizabeth took her responsibilities very seriously and rarely let her hair down even among friends. Margaret didn't care who she shocked and seemed to take a perverse pleasure in showing her emotions.

In their teenage years it was Elizabeth who had to try harder in most things. For Margaret, everything seemed to fall into her lap as if she didn't have to try at all. Most of their circle believed that she was the cleverer of the two and whenever they attended a party together Margaret was always the centre of attention. Elizabeth did not resent her sister's personal popularity but it would not have been natural if she had not felt privately a little piqued at the way she was forced to spend part of every day studying the business of monarchy. There was so much to learn and her father taught her the importance of having at her fingertips the names and titles of most of the world leaders she would meet, how to recognise various decorations and also the stultifying minutiae of constitutional history. While all this was going on, Margaret was enjoying herself, being entertained – and indulged – by her parents, and by just about everybody else with whom she came in contact.

Elizabeth knew she had the respect and admiration of her mother and father, but she suspected that Margaret, as the baby of the family, was the one who enjoyed their unqualified love and devotion. Margaret, on the other hand, was always aware that no matter how glamorous she was, all she would ever be was a princess. Her sister was going to be Queen and Margaret would always be required to take second place. In all probability, the King and Queen did overcompensate in paying attention to Princess Margaret, because they knew that Elizabeth was one day going to become

The two sisters join their mother as she stops to meet a disabled child. Princess Margaret, sheltering under an umbrella, The Queen and Queen Elizabeth the Queen Mother, all clutching small bouquets of flowers as a lady-in-waiting hovers behind to carry the others that are always offered by wellwishers. (Jayne Fincher/© Photographers International)

the most important woman in the country and Margaret would then have to curtsy to her own sister.

But there was one way in which the King and Queen were very strict with Margaret. They would not under any circumstances permit her to show any sign of jealousy or anger in public. And Margaret, to be fair, obeyed this cardinal rule to the letter. If she did have any feelings of resentment towards her sister, no one ever saw it manifested. They were a loving and affectionate pair and as they grew older they appeared to grow even fonder of each other. Princess Margaret would never hear a word spoken against The Queen, and no member of the Royal Family ever heard a whisper of disapproval of Princess Margaret's unconventional behaviour from The Queen. Their loyalty to each other was total and unqualified.

If there is one characteristic that The Queen inherited from her mother it is that she is completely non-judgemental. When her only daughter became divorced from her first husband and she saw the break-up of the marriages of two of her sons, she must have experienced deep sadness. But once the decisions had been made and were irrevocable, she accepted them. Similarly, she could have been involved in one of the most difficult decisions of her reign when Princess Margaret was considering marrying Peter Townsend, when she would have had to decide whether or not to give her consent. As history has recorded, no such decision was necessary as Princess Margaret took matters into her own hands and decided not to marry, but even then there were no angry scenes between The Queen and her sister.

Although The Queen and Princess Margaret had many differences – Margaret's unconventional lifestyle and her total disregard for the opinions of others caused her sister embarrassment and unhappiness – they never held each other in anything but loving respect and admiration. The Queen may have felt that Margaret should have curbed her flamboyant affairs and behaved more as she (Elizabeth) felt she should have as one of the most senior members of the Royal Family, but no one in their immediate circle ever heard a word of criticism escape from The Queen's lips. Similarly, Margaret was heard many times to curse other members of the family, particularly when she heard that one of her near neighbours in Kensington Palace was being openly disapproving of her. But she never once criticised her sister – and neither would she allow anyone else, family or otherwise, to do so. She once rounded on a male fellow guest at a dinner party who had the temerity to enquire after the health of 'your sister'. 'Are you referring to The Queen?' she replied icily, and froze him out for the rest of the evening.

After Princess Margaret suffered her first stroke and was brought back to Britain from the West Indies, she and The Queen became even closer than they had been for years. The Queen realised that her sister's lifestyle had contributed to her sudden decline and she also knew that perhaps it was the beginning of the end. They spoke on the telephone every day and The Queen visited Margaret at least once a week, when the younger sister would surprise Elizabeth by telling her the latest gossip about their friends and the public figures they both knew. Even when she was bedridden,

Margaret still retained her circle of friends who kept her informed of what was going on and by whom, and she knew that Elizabeth loved to hear these stories, the more indelicate the better.

The sisters, with their mother, formed a triumvirate that appeared to need no one else. Margaret, in her seventies, growing increasingly frail in her body but still active mentally; the Queen Mother, having passed her hundredth birthday, was also somewhat shaky on her legs but again there was nothing wrong with her mind, and The Queen, of course, the healthiest of the three. They were a loving family unit; the ancient matriarch and her two daughters, one of whom had once been regarded as one of the most beautiful women in the world, the other, now the most famous woman on earth. They were a formidable team and as The Queen realised that soon she would be the only survivor, she made sure that she lost no opportunity to spend as much time as possible with her mother and sister.

February 2002 and The Queen, with her nephew, David, Viscount Linley, and niece, Lady Sara Chatto, pay their respects as the coffin of Princess Margaret leaves St George's Chapel, Windsor Castle on its final journey. Princess Margaret died at the age of 71. (Fiona Hanson/PA/ EMPICS)

There is nothing sadder for a mother than that her child should die before her. When Princess Margaret died in 2002, the Queen Mother was naturally heartbroken and The Queen's grief equalled her mother's. In the early days following Margaret's death, Elizabeth was inconsolable, with only Prince Philip able to fully understand what the loss meant to his wife. But the business of monarchy had to continue and Her Majesty put on her

public face and carried on her duties without once allowing her private feelings to show. But photographs taken at Princess Margaret's funeral at Windsor Castle clearly indicate the depth of emotion she was suffering.

The Queen has always had a particular affection for her nephew and niece, Princess Margaret's children by Lord Snowdon: David, Viscount Linley, and his sister Lady Sarah Chatto. They are great favourites and Her Majesty thoroughly approved the way in which they both conducted themselves, privately and in public. She also liked the fact that neither had traded on their Royal connections to live a hedonistic lifestyle, and as their father had remained firm friends with both The Queen and his former wife, until her death, this brought the Snowdon children even closer to The Queen and Prince Philip. Anyone who saw the images of David and Sarah at the funeral service of their mother, could not but be moved by their obvious grief and also by the sympathetic expression on the face of The Queen as she accompanied them inside St George's Chapel.

The Queen follows the coffin containing the body of her mother at the funeral service in Westminster Abbey on 9 April 2002. Behind Her Majesty from left to right are: Prince William; the Earl of Wessex, the Prince of Wales and Prince Harry.
(PA/EMPICS)

David and Sarah, and their respective spouses and children, are always welcome at all of The Queen's homes and Her Majesty and Prince Philip know that equally there is an open door at the houses of their nephew and niece.

For anyone to lose both her only sister and her mother in the space of a few short weeks would be a great sadness at any time. When the one remaining is The Queen, who occupies perhaps the loneliest position in the world, the grief and sense of loss can only be imagined, as she never shows her emotions in public.

The death of the Queen Mother just six weeks after that of Princess Margaret was not unexpected; after all she was 102 years old. But she seemed indestructible, having survived numerous operations in old age and telling anyone who would listen, even when she passed the century mark, that 'If you ignore illness it will go away.'

For The Queen, it truly was the end of an era. Her father, sister and now her mother, all gone. The Queen Mother had always been there; not just for The Queen but for most of the population of the country, and while hundreds of thousands of men, women and children turned out to pay their last respects, there was not the outpouring of grief and emotion that was felt when, for example, Diana, Princess of Wales had died so suddenly. Of course, Diana was a comparatively young woman; the Queen Mother was at the end of her natural life. Nevertheless, for The Queen it was an occasion of great personal sadness and loss. She had lost the one woman to whom she could say anything, and nearly every Sunday morning since then she has had cause to remember her mother, as that was when they invariably met over a drink at Royal Lodge in Windsor to discuss the previous day's racing. It is a gap that can never be filled.

The Queen has spoken briefly about the mutual love and respect between herself, the Queen Mother and Princess Margaret. She is not a demonstrative woman but no one who knows her doubts for a moment the depth of those feelings.

And it was Princess Margaret who paid Elizabeth the ultimate compliment when she summed up their relationship succinctly and perfectly, saying, 'Even if she were not my sister, I would still like her to be my best friend.'

twelve

A Woman of *Faith*

In the same way that none of The Queen's prime ministers has ever had an inkling of her politics, in spite of the weekly Tuesday audience when no one else is present, no man who has served her as Archbishop of Canterbury can place his hand on his heart and claim truthfully that he knows her opinions of himself or the Church.

The present incumbent, Dr Rowan Williams, did not have the easiest of introductions as Primate. In his first few months he had to discuss with The Queen – the Supreme Governor of the Church of England, and a rigid traditionalist in most things, particularly her religion – the potentially thorny problems associated with homosexual priests, the ordination of women, and in 2005, the appointment of the Church of England's first black bishop at York and the controversial marriage of the Prince of Wales and Mrs Camilla Parker Bowles.

Two of Archbishop Williams's predecessors had learned that The Queen had no particular problems with homosexual priests as long as they were not too blatant in parading their sexuality, though the Duke of Edinburgh was thought to be not so relaxed. Where women priests were concerned though, Her Majesty was believed to have had reservations. As one who had never previously challenged the status quo when all Church of England clergy were male, she felt there was no need for change, but, being a realist, she understood that she had to accept the place of women in the

Church, even if reluctantly. Still, the Court Circular rarely lists women priests as preaching in churches attended by The Queen. On the question of black bishops, Her Majesty welcomes the appointment. She is totally unprejudiced and regards race as an irrelevance, but it has been pointed out that at the time of writing no black or Asian man or woman has yet been appointed to a senior position in her Household.

Various archbishops have mistakenly imagined that they enjoyed a special relationship with the Supreme Governor of the Church of England – and that is what she is, not the Head of the Church as is so often incorrectly reported. But as the former Archbishop of Canterbury, the late Robert Runcie, said, 'It's all in the mind. You are there because of your position and not because she has taken a particular fancy to you. Once you leave the post, you quickly find you are out of mind and the next man has moved in. It's a very salutary experience as so many of us imagined that we played a very important role in The Queen's life and enjoyed a special relationship.'

One thing all her archbishops have been agreed upon though is that The Queen's Christian belief is central to her life and always

The Queen is flanked by the Archbishop of Canterbury, Dr Rowan Williams, and the President of the Methodist Conference as they stand in front of a statue of John Wesley. The occasion was a service for the signing of an Anglican–Methodist Covenant after more than two centuries of separation over episcopal authority and ordination. (Kirsty Wigglesworth/PA/ EMPICS)

has been. Nothing shakes her faith and for her the Coronation was a religious experience. When she was anointed she accepted her role as being for the rest of her life. There will be no abdication in spite of the fact that she is already twenty years over the normal retiring age for women. She believes that the oath she took on 2 June 1953 in Westminster Abbey is as binding today as it was fifty-three years ago and her faith has sustained her through years of private turmoil, particularly when the marriages of three of her children ended in divorce. As a mother she must have felt she was partly to blame for these failures. Similarly, the deaths of her younger sister, Princess Margaret, and, six weeks later, her mother caused her to suffer great personal pain which was only partly relieved by her adherence to her Christian beliefs.

The Queen may not question Christianity as such, but she has not always agreed with her Archbishops of Canterbury on matters of dogma or the way the Church has been modernising in recent years.

She was once taken to a church in the East End of London where the vicar had introduced an evangelical side to his services, much to the approval of his congregation. As she left, The Queen murmured that he obviously had his finger on the pulse of the people he was serving, 'But I think I'll stay with the traditional form I'm used to.'

To possess a faith that is so unquestioning must be a source of great comfort to anyone; when that person is a woman in a position as isolated as The Queen's, it is even more so. Prince Philip is also a man of faith but, unlike his wife, he questions everything about religion. His correspondence with the former Dean of Windsor, the Revd Michael Mann, was published in the 1980s and reveals the depth of his feelings and his need to be convinced on the subject of Christianity in relation to science and morality, matters that many Christians accept simply because the Church tells them to. It was Prince Philip who intervened when the Church hierarchy wanted the Dean removed at one time. Philip wouldn't have it and 'persuaded' the authorities to think again. It is believed he was fully supported by The Queen. Prince Philip's practical interest in religious affairs came to public notice when he established St George's College at Windsor in 1966 as a forum for serious religious discussion.

To The Queen, her religion is a very private affair. She does not trumpet her beliefs and when she takes holy communion, it is not at a public service. On Sunday mornings, she receives communion from her chaplain in the privacy of her own chapel at Windsor, before attending morning service with other worshippers. The Queen Mother and Princess Margaret shared her beliefs and they also preferred to accept the sacrament without the presence of other churchgoers.

Prayer is another aspect of Her Majesty's Anglican religion that she practises on a daily basis, but again, in private. She does attend the usual church services – at Sandringham, Windsor, and Crathie when she is staying at Balmoral – and she is passed the collection plate in the same way as everyone else. But, because Her Majesty does not carry money, her equerry, who sits immediately behind her, passes her a newly minted £10 note just before the collection reaches her.

Prince Philip will occasionally read the lesson in church; The Queen has never done so, and she has let it be known that she prefers not to be asked.

Visiting clergy (four bishops are invited) who are asked to preach at Sandringham and the other churches used by the Royal Family are instructed to keep their sermons brief and simple. Prince Philip will not tolerate lengthy and boring sermons. As he once put it: 'The mind and soul cannot absorb what the buttocks cannot bear.' On those few occasions when preachers have spoken for too long, his icy glare and noisy snorts usually make them get the message rather quickly.

The Queen never expresses an opinion either way, but privately she is believed to be not too displeased that her husband takes this attitude.

The Queen has a remarkable memory and several of her Archbishops of Canterbury have been surprised when she has recalled something one of them mentioned in a sermon preached more than a year previously. One archbishop thought it might have something to do with self-taught training in dealing with the thousands of government papers that pass through her hands every year. Another said it was more likely to be because of her passion for horse racing and the way in which she has developed a photographic memory regarding results and blood lines of the horses in her stables.

There has never been a time when The Queen did not take religion seriously. She was brought up in a committed Christian family and when she was 15 she was prepared for confirmation by the then Dean of Windsor, Canon Crawley. He also instructed her younger sister, but Margaret was not in the least interested in the teachings of the Church at that time, so she did not pay too much attention to his words. Of course, later in life, Princess Margaret became intensely religious and even at one time said she was considering converting to the Roman Catholic faith.

Princess Elizabeth had always taken her churchgoing and prayer seriously so she was fully prepared when she was confirmed in the private chapel at Windsor Castle on 28 March 1942, when the Second World War was at its height and Britain was facing severe difficulties. The confirmation was conducted by the Archbishop of Canterbury, Cosmo Gordon Lang, and the event was considered to be so important that Elizabeth's grandmother, Queen Mary, came to Windsor from her self-imposed wartime exile at Badminton, the home of the Duke of Beaufort. Although Princess Margaret was confirmed at the same time, hardly any mention was made of her presence; all eyes were on Elizabeth, the future Queen.

In years to come The Queen made sure all her children and grandchildren were also confirmed in the Anglican faith – and all by Archbishops of Canterbury. She didn't always agree with her archbishops

The late Pope John Paul II greets The Queen and Prince Philip during a visit to the Vatican in 1980. His Holiness became firm friends with the Royal couple and they made a return visit twenty years later. The Pope was also a guest at Buckingham Palace. (TopFoto.co.uk)

though. When Prince William's christening was being planned, she suggested to Lord Runcie, the then Archbishop of Canterbury, that it might be nice to mix the old and new forms of the service. He told her it would be highly irregular and she backed down saying she did not want any special arrangements made on her behalf.

One argument she did win was over the colour of the cassocks worn by clergy and choristers at Exeter Cathedral. When she visited the cathedral she found they were wearing red cassocks and she said she understood only those clergy and servers at the Royal Peculiars – Canterbury and Westminster Abbey – were permitted to wear scarlet. Exeter declined to change, pointing to ancient documents that gave them permission. In the end a compromise was reached when The Queen agreed to pay for new cassocks – but not in red.

Her Majesty does not like to compromise, and for much of the time she does not have to, but in ecclesiastical matters she sometimes has to bend to the advice of her Archbishop of Canterbury as she did in 1981 when the then Prime Minister, Margaret Thatcher, nominated Graham Leonard to be Bishop of London in preference to John Hapgood, The Queen's choice. It was the late Robert Runcie, as Archbishop of Canterbury, who had the delicate task of informing Her Majesty that the decision had been made and could not be changed.

The appointment of bishops is made by The Queen on the advice of the Prime Minister to whom two names are submitted by a selection board called the Crown Appointments Committee. If Her Majesty has a good reason for not approving the appointment she can ask for more information or even another name, but as a constitutional monarch, she is obliged to accept the advice of her Prime Minister in this, as in all official appointments. It is during the swearing-in of a new bishop that the position of The Queen as Supreme Governor of the Church of England is publicly acknowledged. As the Home Secretary recites the oath of allegiance (which is to Her Majesty, not to the Archbishop of Canterbury or any other higher authority), she clasps the bishop's hands between her own to signify her acceptance of his pledge. In other words, that he is her bishop and she alone has the power to appoint and remove him. But again, in reality, it would have to be with the agreement of the Prime Minister.

Among the most difficult times for The Queen have been the divorces of her sister and three of her children and, of course, the civil second

Every year since she first came to the throne, The Queen has attended services in cathedrals up and down Britain to hand out Maundy Money. It is a centuries-old tradition whereby gift purses containing coins – representing each year of the Sovereign's life – are given to deserving men and women. Since 1971, the coins have been decimal currency and are now the only silver coins still being minted.
(Phil Noble/PA/ EMPICS)

wedding of Prince Charles (see Chapter Four – Happy the Bride?). As a traditional Protestant with a firm and unshakeable Christian belief, these events caused her immense personal sadness, and as Sovereign, enormous concern over the constitutional problems posed by the marriage of her son and heir to a divorced woman. As Monarch, she would have preferred Prince Charles not to have married Camilla Parker Bowles as his eventual succession would then have been seamless. But as a mother, she obviously wanted her eldest child to be happy and he was determined to wed the woman he loved anyway, so she made the best of it.

In the eyes of Elizabeth II, personal happiness comes a poor second to public duty every time. The discussions between Her Majesty and the Archbishop of Canterbury over this thorny subject will probably remain secret forever.

She is an entirely orthodox Christian whose commitment is as unqualified today as it was when she was a young girl. Those who know her best say she may not wear her religion on her sleeve, but as she enters her ninth decade, it is her faith that has sustained her through good times and bad.

thirteen

The Queen
and the
Arts

It is said in Palace circles that The Queen has never read a detective story, romantic novel or comedy in her life. The only books she reads and which interest her are those about horses. If this is true, it is remarkable that she has become so well informed about literature and the arts, without having read any of the standard works.

Every year she is presented with copies of new books by well-meaning authors, every one of which has been personally inscribed with the words 'Dedicated to Her Majesty with respectful good wishes' and signed by the author. Each one will be acknowledged, the book added to the Royal library – and forgotten. The exception, in terms of fiction, are the novels of Dick Francis, who was formerly the Queen Mother's jockey and who always made sure Her Majesty received the first copy of every new book he wrote. Dick Francis's books are all thrillers but every one has an equestrian theme running through it.

The Queen has a reputation for not being particularly enthusiastic about any single one of the arts. If she goes to the theatre it is because she is expected to attend, not because there is a show she wants to see. She does not care for ballet and grand opera holds no fascination for her as it does for Prince Charles. The Royal Variety Show is an annual chore she is expected to attend as Patron, and while she never shirks her responsibilities, everyone in the Royal

Household knows she finds most of the acts boring in the extreme. She does enjoy some television and still watches old tapes of the detective series *Morse* starring the late John Thaw, a great favourite. She also used to enjoy the long-running quiz show *Countdown* on Channel 4. Indeed, she was reported to be quite vexed when the time of the programme was brought forward as it then clashed with her walk in the Palace grounds with her corgis. Her staff say she is not impressed with the current crop of television offerings and 'alternative' comedy leaves her cold, but she has been heard to giggle at the irreverence of Dawn French's Vicar of Dibley and she is said to believe that David Suchet's portrayal of Agatha Christie's Belgian detective Hercule Poirot, is the best yet.

Notwithstanding the barbed comments of one or two critics, Her Majesty does take an interest in her own art collection, which is arguably the finest in the world with 7,000 paintings, 30,000 drawings and watercolours,

The Queen meeting members of the cast of the Royal Variety Performance, 21 November 2005. (Austin Hargrave/PA/EMPICS)

3,000 miniatures and 500,000 engravings, making a total, including furniture and other artefacts, of over 1 million items, but in the main she leaves the details of the Royal Collection to the department in the Royal Household that bears its name. The Royal Collection Department, housed in St James's Palace, is now the largest of the six Household departments and looks after items worth hundreds of millions of pounds. It is run by a Board of Trustees, chaired by the Prince of Wales with Lord Luce, the Lord Chamberlain, as his deputy and with The Queen's Private Secretary, Sir Robin Janvrin, and the Director of the Royal Collection on its board.

The Royal Collection has some 350 permanent staff employed in its various subdivisions, which is swollen considerably by the number of part-timers and temporary staff who come in to act as wardens during the summer opening of Buckingham Palace. In addition, they also run the Royal shops in the precincts of all the Royal residences through Royal Collection Enterprises, the commercial arm of the department, and they are responsible for the Crown Jewels, housed in the Tower of London. It is a proud boast of the Collection that it is the only part of the Royal Household to be profitable year after year. It is run very much as a business with one of its most profitable lines being the loan – for fees – of photographic copies of its vast collection of works of art. Newspapers, magazines and television companies all over the world constantly enquire about borrowing copies of some of the most famous works and the Royal Archives, which is part of the Royal Collection, now issues a standard set of fees ranging from £30 for a black and white illustration to be used only on the inside of a book or magazine with less than 5,000 copies, to £320 for the same in colour. Charges for jacket pictures are correspondingly higher.

The Queen also insists that publishers should not show just a part of a photograph of her. So, for instance, if someone wants to show a particular diamond from a tiara, or a ring, they have to include the entire picture. They are not allowed to show the jewellery alone, without Her Majesty.

It comes as a surprise to many people to learn that there are over 2,500 transparencies in the Royal Collection; each one numbered and catalogued. And part of the job of the Administrator of the Royal Collection is to keep an up-to-date list and accurate description of every item of jewellery, including tiaras, collars, earrings and cufflinks, owned by each member of the Royal Family. This is done so that in the event of loss or damage, the Crown Jewellers, Asprey or Garrard, can replace or repair the item without delay.

The present Director of the Royal Collection is Sir Hugh Roberts, a distinguished expert in several fields of the arts, and acknowledged throughout the world to be a leader in his field. He is the latest in a line that includes several colourful characters such as Kenneth (later Lord) Clark, father of the outspoken politician Alan Clark, and the most notorious, Sir Anthony Blunt, who was revealed to have been spying for the Russians during the Cold War.

Sir Hugh is a much more conventional appointment and among the questions he is frequently asked is how large is The Queen's private collection and does she own all the works of art in the Royal Collection? By now he has answered the queries so often, the replies have become almost automatic.

The Royal Collection is essentially the historic collection, assembled over some 500 years and held in trust by The Queen as Sovereign for her successors and the nation. She does not own it as a private individual. She has acquired items specifically for the Collection and she does own a number of her own private works of art, which are distinct from the Royal Collection. This means, of course, that although she holds the major part of the Royal Collection in trust for her successors, she cannot sell any of them for her own benefit. They are regarded as inalienable.

The Queen viewing the Crown Jewels at the Tower of London after performing the opening ceremony at the new £10 million jewel house at the tower, March 1994. (Sean Dempsey/PA/EMPICS)

Among the items Her Majesty has acquired since she came to the throne in 1952 are a number associated with her own Coronation in 1953. She has bought the Coronation bouquet by Anna Zinkeisen and the Coronation dress and robe of estate; the dress is by Sir Norman Hartnell and the robe by the Royal School of Needlework. She also obtained a painting by Sir Herbert James Gunn, entitled 'Queen Elizabeth II in Coronation Robes'.

The earliest artefact The Queen owns is described as a 'Hunting sword, by-knife and scabbard' by Diego de Caias and is dated 1544, while she also liked – and bought – a portrait of her ill-fated ancestor, Charles I, painted in 1628 by Daniel Mytens. Anything connected with previous Royalty, or Royal homes, is of personal interest to Her Majesty and she has acquired paintings of rooms in Windsor Castle and Osborne House, the favourite home of her great-great-grandmother Queen Victoria.

A source in the Royal Collection told me that The Queen is very aware of modern trends. In 2004 she sat for a holographic portrait by Chris Levine and she has also been painted by Lucien Freud – a controversial picture that attracted severe criticism when it was displayed in The Queen's Gallery at Buckingham Palace but which she, nevertheless, acquired for her private collection.

There are constant calls on her to sit for portraits and if she considers this to be an irritation, she keeps her thoughts very much to herself, regarding it as part of her role to make herself accessible to artists. Some of the 'purists' were dismayed when they heard that she had agreed to sit for Rolf Harris, better known for his comedy and musical talent on television, but who has proved himself to be an artist with great popular appeal, and the fact that The Queen obviously realises this has revealed that she is prepared to give her time to someone who is not one of the more conventionally accepted Royal artists. However, before she agreed to the sittings – and there have been many – she took the advice of her Surveyor of The Queen's Pictures, and also of Prince Philip, both of whom obviously thought it was a good idea. It has certainly been excellent public relations and helped to dispel the stuffy image of Royal art.

As with The Queen's acquisition of thoroughbreds to add to her racing stables, she seeks the advice of experts to help her choose any new additions to the Royal Collection. The men who run the Collection regard it as part of their role to alert her to an item that might be of interest and an appropriate acquisition. But she does not always take their advice. If she does not like a particular painting, objet d'art or piece of furniture, she will not sanction its purchase, even if it is a bargain and bound to increase in value. And the Director and his staff know that the final decision is hers and she will not change her mind once it is made up.

Many people think that The Queen has a bottomless pocket and can buy anything she wants without thinking of the cost. But with works of art in the international market now fetching, in some cases, tens of millions of pounds at auction, collectors such as Lord Lloyd Webber, Britain's most successful musical composer and impresario, and Bill Gates, one of the world's richest men, with a fortune estimated to be over $30 billion, can outbid The Queen with ease.

During her reign, The Queen has insisted on making her Collection more widely accessible. She has created two new galleries, at Buckingham Palace and in a beautifully converted church at the foot of Edinburgh's Royal Mile. The total cost was £23 million, without the support of any public or lottery funding. And as the Royal Collection is entirely self-funded, she can only buy when resources are available. In this, of course, she is not alone. Every gallery and national museum finds itself in the same situation in this increasingly competitive market.

One of the Royal Collection's leading experts explained that The Queen asks them to keep a special eye open for anything she might like to add to her Collection. But not all the new items have been bought by her – or on her behalf – on the advice of her Household. Many she first heard about from friends and family, particularly when Queen Elizabeth the Queen Mother was alive, as she was an avid collector and would often tell her daughter about something she had seen or heard about and that she felt would appeal.

Occasionally items that have a very strong association with the Royal Collection or the Royal Family become available on the market and those who buy for Her Majesty are told to bid. In 2004 The Queen acquired an important Sevres vase, which was the missing centrepiece of a garniture of three vases purchased by Marie-Antoinette in 1779 for Versailles. The flanking vases, which had probably become separated from the centre vase in the aftermath of the French Revolution, were already in the Royal Collection, having been bought by George IV (reigned 1820–30). So the acquisition of the remaining centrepiece completed the set.

One of the difficulties is that once someone knows The Queen is interested, the price shoots up, so she never bids in her own name and neither does anyone from the Royal Collection do so on her behalf. They use independent art dealers including Hazlitt, Gooden and Fox, one of

London's most reputable companies, who buy and sell for Her Majesty. And when they do enter the market on her behalf they also include items from other clients so that no one knows exactly who they are acting for.

In 2003 The Queen managed to obtain a unique Sevres porcelain dessert service, made in 1789 to mark George III's recovery from his first serious bout of porphyria. Again, the tea and coffee sets were already in the Collection and it was a matter of great satisfaction to Her Majesty that her new acquisition could be reunited with the other parts of the service for the first time in over 200 years.

Among other items bought by The Queen is a painting of the author Graham Greene, completed in 1989 by Humphrey Ocean, and a magnificent writing desk designed by Ernst Anton Plischke between 1947 and 1949. So her tastes are quite eclectic.

Certain art critics like to claim that The Queen is an ignoramus or Philistine when it comes to her own art collection. Her choice of paintings and drawings for her own private apartments suggests differently. At Buckingham Palace she has a magnificent Canaletto that has been a favourite for many years, as well as a John Piper left to her by the Queen Mother; Prince Charles has other John Piper works that were owned by his grandmother at Clarence House. The Queen enjoys looking at sketches of her corgis, little vignettes, and there is a beautiful painting of three horse's heads by Susan Crawford. The Queen chose all these personally and no one who has had the pleasure of being invited into the private apartments would quarrel with her selection. All the paintings and drawings are reasonably small, at least compared with some of the massive Van Dycks in the State Apartments, and they contribute to the atmosphere of domesticity in the rooms which are comfortable if not sumptuous.

Another aspect of The Queen's involvement in the arts is the way she allows many of her treasures to be made available to other institutions, in some cases on permanent loan, so that members of the public can have access to works of art that previously were restricted to a very few, privileged insiders. The prime stipulation is that the borrowers must satisfy the Royal Collection that they have premises that are sufficiently secure and with suitable facilities for display. And, of course, substantial insurance policies must be taken out in case of loss or damage. Strangely, The Queen's own collection is not insured because she feels that if something is truly irreplaceable, there is little point.

While her interest in the Royal Collection has been described as 'sporadic' and she would much prefer a day at the races or even at the Royal stables than a few hours in the National Gallery, The Queen does take her responsibilities as Patron of the Arts as seriously as all her other duties. It is just that, as with all of us, she finds certain duties 'less interesting' than others. I have spoken to a number of Royal Collection staff and as they were not being quoted, they were at liberty to say what they felt about their boss. The general consensus seems to be that while The Queen does not have a great passion for the arts, she does take an intelligent interest and she is extremely well informed. Above all, she appreciates what she's got.

* * *

Probably one of the most jealously guarded aspects of The Queen's life is her contributions to charity. As Sovereign, she is inundated with requests for money, time and artefacts to raise funds for a wide variety of causes. Obviously she cannot accede to them all and Buckingham Palace does not issue an official list of the charities with which Her Majesty is associated. But inevitably news leaks out on occasion when she does contribute to something she considers to be particularly worthwhile, or which has touched her emotionally. The Aberfan Disaster of 1966 when 144 people, including 116 children, were killed after a coal tip collapsed, engulfing the village school, was one such case. The Queen and Prince Philip visited the site a few days after the event and when the Aberfan Memorial Fund was established, a member of the committee revealed, without consulting the Palace, that Her Majesty had made a substantial contribution.

Similarly, in 1996 when an unstable man walked into a schoolroom in Dunblane in Scotland and shot and killed a teacher and sixteen children, before killing himself, The Queen, accompanied by the Princess Royal, went to the school four days later to mourn with the villagers and parents and to offer their sympathy. The Queen's sympathy took a more practical slant later when she again gave money to help the bereaved villagers.

Of course, not all Her Majesty's help for charities is the result of tragedy. Every year she attends the Royal Variety Performance and the Royal Film Performance, both of which are held in aid of charity. She has also donated

The Queen and Prince Philip visited Aberfan in South Wales a few days after a coal tip had collapsed onto the village school, killing 144 people including 116 children. She was visibly distressed at the sights that met her and spent several hours comforting bereaved parents. (Stan Meagher/*Express*/Getty Images)

the entire Royal Music Library, containing 7,000 pieces of music, to the British Museum.

Many of The Queen's charitable organisations are concerned with youth. She acts as Patron of the Boy Scouts Association and she has contacts with several schools in and around the Royal homes. For instance, every year she presents a bible to Dersingham School near Sandringham, to the pupil who has excelled in religious knowledge. She also acts as Patron of the Star and Garter Homes for Disabled Sailors, Soldiers and Airmen, which helps any ex-serviceman or woman who has been physically disabled for any reason, and the Friends of the Clergy Corporation, another organisation that provides assistance for men and women in distressed circumstances. The people who manage these charities will, on occasion, bring to The Queen's notice a particularly deserving case and she has a private fund out of which help is always forthcoming.

Many of the individuals and organisations she assists would like to make the fact public but The Queen is adamant that one condition she insists upon when making a gift, is total anonymity – even to the recipients. The amount of money she gives is never disclosed, but when a charity does acknowledge her contribution they will occasionally reveal that it is 'very generous'.

fourteen

The Queen
at 80

Tony Blair once said that there were only two people in the world to whom a prime minister can say what he feels about his Cabinet colleagues without fear that his words will be repeated. One is his wife and the other is The Queen.

Most of the Blair Cabinet – and his wife, Cherie – are believed to be republicans at heart, and during his terms of office, he himself has introduced legislation to curtail the role of the monarchy in the United Kingdom. It was Tony Blair who encouraged devolution for Scotland and Wales, with Scotland being granted a full Parliament of its own, and Wales making do with a Welsh Assembly. The Queen, understandably, does not relish the idea of any break-up of Britain, but as a constitutional monarch there was nothing she could do to prevent it. She did perform both opening ceremonies, in Edinburgh and Cardiff, and she also opened the exciting but controversial new Scottish Parliament building, designed by the Spanish architect Enric Miralles, in October 2004.

On all these occasions, with her usual flawless professionalism, no one could guess from her demeanour what her true feelings were. We still have no idea which party she would support if she were allowed to vote. But it doesn't take much of an educated guess to suppose she would not wholeheartedly approve her government's headlong rush into closer involvement in Europe, which would inevitably reduce the role and power of the Sovereign in Britain.

The Queen's sense of duty and devotion to her people has remained unchanged in over half a century and has stayed as her ideal throughout her life. Her Majesty is a realist who knows that compromises are necessary if the monarchy is to be seen to move with the times but she does not welcome the downgrading of certain aspects of her role, either in Britain or throughout the Commonwealth. Prince William, who will be crowned as King William V (if he keeps his own name) at some time this century, has already indicated that he finds much of the pomp and pageantry of the present-day institution distasteful. It is an attitude that may well find favour among the younger element in the land, but The Queen feels that scaling down the sort of grandiose spectacular occasions that people have come to expect of Royalty during her reign could further isolate the Royal Family from an increasingly indifferent public. She knows better than most, that ceremonial activity helps maintain the high profile of the monarchy and has never neglected her role as a highly visible Head of State.

Aware as she is of the importance of ceremony in her public life, Her Majesty – like her father before her – cannot be equalled in her knowledge of the protocol required for the different occasions. Several officers have been reminded by her that they are perhaps wearing medals in the wrong order, or riding too close to her carriage when they are on escort duty. But it is not arrogance that prompts her to tell them that the people have come to see her not them. Privately she is very modest with a complete lack of vanity. Her couturier Maureen Rose says she only looks in a mirror to check that everything is as it should be, not because she wants to see how good she looks.

At the same time, she has accepted with her usual grace the changed circumstances of a once all-powerful position, without in any way lowering her own high standards. We live in a world that is less reverential and deferential than it was in the 1950s, and public interest in the Royals has declined sharply in recent years. But another of Her Majesty's former prime ministers,

Opposite: At the State Opening of Parliament The Queen reads a speech from the throne in the House of Lords outlining the government's legislative programme for the coming year. She does not write any part of the speech; that is the responsibility of the prime minister. (Matthew Fearn/PA/EMPICS)

Sir John Major, who was invited by The Queen to become a Knight of the Garter, the highest Order of Chivalry, in June 2005, will never hear a word spoken against her. He was only 8 years old when she came to the throne and was also her youngest Prime Minister, at 47, until Tony Blair arrived at No. 10. He found her to be a constant source of encouragement and, like Mr Blair, said he could say anything to Her Majesty, even things he could not confide to his Cabinet colleagues. Major was and is a confirmed monarchist and when The Queen and Prince Charles agreed, in 1992, to pay income tax for the first time, he said, 'I detect no enthusiasm in this country for anything other than a continuation of the constitutional monarchy.'

One royal trait The Queen has inherited from generations of her family is never to discuss any topic that is awkward or embarrassing. Her parents would never dream of talking about family problems even in private, and The Queen is exactly the same. She shies away from subjects that might prove difficult, unlike Prince Philip, to whom nothing is sacrosanct. He will engage in discussions and arguments with anyone on practically any topic. When Prince Charles approached his mother with news of his separation and divorce, The Queen would not have shown to her son any fears she might have had, for, together with nearly every other member of the Royal Family, she finds it difficult to show emotion, either in public or even with her family. Prince Philip is the only person in the world with whom Her Majesty can be completely relaxed. Everyone else, even her own children, is kept at arm's length.

This inability to show emotion was never better illustrated than in 1995 at the fiftieth VE Day anniversary celebrations in Hyde Park. The ceremony was attended by Heads of State from all over the world and part of the proceedings involved each of these Heads of State being led to the Globe of Peace by a child, representing the future. Every great man or woman held the hand of the little boy or girl who accompanied him or her with one notable exception – The Queen. She alone declined to take the hand of the child alongside her, not because she didn't want to, but because it was alien to her nature. As one of her long-serving aides remarked, 'It simply would not have occurred to her.'

Although it has been suggested that The Queen lives in an ivory tower, protected from the uglier side of life, and that those closest to her tell her only what they think she wants to hear, nothing could be further from the truth. If one of her Private Secretaries did follow this path he would soon find himself working elsewhere. In the early days of her reign, the Court was circumscribed by attitudes that had prevailed for generations and Private Secretaries such as Martin (later Lord) Charteris, did try to make sure nothing untoward reached the Royal ears. But Sir Robin Janvrin and his immediate predecessor, Robert (now Lord) Fellowes, always 'bit the bullet' when they had unpleasant news to impart. They realised they would be doing her no favours by keeping unpleasant details from her and frequently had to face her with news of the latest scandal to hit a member of her family. Fellowes had a particularly tough period as he was brother-in-law to the late Diana, Princess of Wales and it was during his term of office that the separation, divorce and tragic death occurred.

The only occasion when The Queen has found herself to be the target of serious criticism was at the time of the death of Diana, Princess of Wales in 1997. After the initial shock and sense of profound grief that engulfed the nation, extreme anger was directed at the Royal Family in general and The Queen in particular because no flag was seen to be flying at half-mast above Buckingham Palace, always regarded as the fulcrum on occasions of national rejoicing and sadness. This is where the people gather to offer their support or their sympathy – and they expected some outward sign of Royal sorrow.

What few people realised, and even fewer cared, was that when The Queen is not in residence – and she was in Scotland, at Balmoral Castle at the time – no standard of any description was ever flown at Buckingham Palace. The flagpole remained bare. There was no intention of disrespect. The Household were simply following the usual procedure – and on this occasion they got it wrong. However, lessons were learned, for when Islamic fundamentalists set off four bombs in central London on 7 July 2005, killing over fifty people and injuring hundreds, Her Majesty immediately ordered the flag over Buckingham Palace to be flown at half-mast. She also, together with other members of the Royal Family, visited injured survivors in hospital within days, perhaps another lesson learned post-Diana?

But back in 1997, it is likely that at first The Queen was unaware she was being pilloried in the media, despite headlines such as 'Show Us You Care' appearing in the tabloid newspapers. Her Private Secretary,

Three days before Christmas 1988, a bomb exploded over the Scottish town of Lockerbie, on a Boeing 747 flying from Frankfurt to New York, killing all 259 people on board and a further 11 people on the ground. Here The Queen visits the site of the tragedy. (Matthew Polak/CORBIS)

Sir Robert Fellowes, was on duty at the Palace while his deputy, Robin Janvrin, had accompanied The Queen to Balmoral. The Household does not move without consultation and it took several days before Her Majesty ordered a Union Jack to be flown at half-mast over Buckingham Palace in a complete break with tradition. It did not appease the crowds entirely but there was a slight lessening of the feelings of anger towards The Queen. Then when she and Prince Philip did arrive in London they stopped their car outside the gates of Buckingham Palace and were seen looking at the thousands of bouquets of flowers left there in tribute to Diana, and when Princes William and Harry joined the crowds in front of Kensington

Palace, much of the people's natural affection for the Royal Family re-emerged.

But the real triumph occurred when The Queen gave what was easily the most moving speech of her life. On the eve of Diana's funeral, Friday 5 September, speaking on live television to an audience estimated to be over 500 million, in a room at the front of Buckingham Palace with the crowds behind her in The Mall, she spoke with true feeling and sadness about Diana. Using the magic phrase 'speaking as a grandmother' she won the hearts of everyone watching and listening. In those few moments she displayed a wonderful sense of grief and dignity without any false emotion or sentiment and changed the mood of the nation.

In all her previous televised speeches – the annual Christmas broadcast and at the State Opening of Parliament – The Queen had never looked completely comfortable or at ease. And while this was not an occasion for comfort, she did appear to be speaking from the heart and with sincerity. The speech was written for her by Robert Fellowes and had been sent to Downing Street as a matter of courtesy. Tony Blair's press spokesman was later reported to have claimed that he suggested the phrase 'as a grandmother'. If he did, it was a mark of genius and put a human face on the image of monarchy at this most distressing time.

If The Queen lives to be 100 and people are asked to recall significant things she has said, they will probably mention only three: the first will be her broadcast speech from South Africa on the occasion of her twenty-first birthday when she promised to devote her life 'whether it be long or short' to the service of the people. The second would be her speech at the Guildhall in London on 24 November 1992. The Queen was suffering from a cold and a sore throat but she refused to cancel the engagement and let her hosts down. Speaking in a husky tone that emphasised the emotional content of the speech, she talked about her *annus horribilis* as 'not a year I shall look back on with undiluted pleasure'. A masterpiece of Royal understatement as this was the year when her only daughter, Princess Anne, became divorced from Mark Phillips, Prince Andrew and his wife separated, prior to a divorce, and it was already clear that the marriage of the Prince and Princess of Wales was heading the same way. In addition, The Queen had suffered, just a week earlier, seeing her beloved Windsor Castle catch fire causing millions of pounds worth of damage. She presented a lonely figure at the Guildhall, but there still was not an ounce of self-pity in her demeanour.

The third most memorable speech was the one previously mentioned on the evening before the funeral of the late Diana, Princess of Wales. These are the speeches for which I believe she will be remembered most of all.

But she also made a ground-breaking speech at the Guildhall in London at a banquet hosted by the Corporation of London to mark Her Majesty's Golden Jubilee in June 2002. Speaking on behalf of herself and Prince Philip, she paid tribute to their children, saying, 'We both of us have a special place in our hearts for our children. I want to express my admiration for the Prince of Wales and for all he has achieved for this country. Our children and all my family have given me such love and unstinting help over the years, and especially in recent months', an obvious reference to the deaths of the Queen Mother and Princess Margaret. It was the first time The Queen had spoken so openly and movingly about her family and revealed the human face of this very public figure.

Now entering her ninth decade, The Queen is a constant in an ever-changing world. And this is part of the reason for her popularity, even though she has never courted it as such. As one of her longest-serving courtiers once said, 'She is not running for election.'

The former Labour leader, Lord Kinnock, told me that if there were to be an election for a president, The Queen would almost certainly win. He added, 'The British people have shown that they want a monarchy and that they respect The Queen as Sovereign and her husband as Consort.'

He might also have said that in the light of the events of the past year (2005), particularly the controversial marriage of the Prince of Wales to Camilla Parker Bowles, when serious doubts were cast over the suitability of Prince Charles to succeed The Queen, many people will pray that Her Majesty lives for many more years in order to restore and retain the stability of the Royal Family we enjoyed at the beginning of her reign. Her Majesty performs her role brilliantly, and selflessly. It would be to the advantage of her heirs – son and grandson – to follow her example.

Select Bibliography

Among the books consulted were:

Allison, R. and Riddell, S. *The Royal Encyclopedia*, Macmillan, 1991

Bradford, Sarah. *Elizabeth: A Biography of HM The Queen*, Heinemann, 1996

Clinton, Bill. *My Life*, Hutchinson, 2004

Dimbleby, Jonathan. *The Prince of Wales*, Little, Brown, 1994

Flamini, Roland. *Sovereign*, Delocorte Press, 1991

Hoey, Brian. *Mountbatten*, Sidgwick & Jackson, 1994

——. *Her Majesty*, HarperCollins, 2002

Judd, Denis. *Prince Philip*, Michael Joseph, 1980

Lacey, Robert. *Majesty*, Hutchinson, 1977

Longford, Elizabeth. *Elizabeth R*, Weidenfeld & Nicolson, 1983

Pimlott, Ben. The Queen, HarperCollins, 1996

Warwick, Christopher. *Princess Margaret*, Weidenfeld & Nicolson, 1983

Index

Page numbers in *italic* refer to photographs.

Index

Index

Index